Praise for *Goodbye Hiding, Hello Freedom*

Opening and reading this book is like going to coffee with the big sister you never had, but needed! Morgan is an incredible friend to dive into the messiness that sin causes in our life based off of her own story and vulnerability that she shares. She holds your hand and walks you out of the shame life has put on you, and into the loving arms of Jesus. It's a must-read if you are battling the grip of shame.

SADIE ROBERTSON HUFF, speaker and *New York Times* bestselling author, *Live Original*, *Live Fearless*, and *Live*

Morgan offers one of the most precious and personal gifts to women: freedom from shame, as she takes your hand and courageously invites you into the depths of her story, allowing the reader to trust that they are not meant to carry the burden of shame. It is a "with you" read that, like a best friend, reassures you that "it's going to be OK."

ELISABETH HASSELBECK, *New York Times* bestselling author; Emmy award–winning television cohost

Morgan's words are like a faithful companion in the journey from the head to the heart in understanding the truth of our identity in Jesus and the redeeming hand of God in the pages of our lives. She vulnerably shares her story and thoroughly explores the Word, leaving us with riches to treasure. An absolute must-read.

FRANNI RAE CASH CAIN of We The Kingdom

Goodbye Hiding, Hello Freedom delivers a powerful, chain-breaking message that every woman needs to hear. The words on these pages tell a story of how God can redeem our brokenness and point to a Savior that unconditionally loves you. Whether it's your past or a current struggle holding you back from experiencing true freedom, I challenge you to read this book and let the truths Morgan presents saturate your soul and let her story of freedom from shame become you

JAMIE HEARD, Founder and Executive Women

T0205019

Morgan writes with relatability, truth, and each page pointed me to God's presence. This book is a guide and tool all young women need. I love her focus on helping us find freedom. I have felt the weight of shame, but reading Morgan's work reminded me just how beautiful freedom in Christ is, and the goodness it gives us in this chaotic world.

GRACE VALENTINE, author of *Am I Enough?*, *Is It Just Me?*, and *What Will They Think?*

With empathy, transparency, and the power of God's Word, Morgan meets the reader where she is and shows her the freedom that is found in Jesus. No matter where you are or what your past entails, this book will encourage you in the truth of God's character and help you say "good-bye" to shame and "hello" to the redemption God made a way for you to personally know.

EMMA MAE MCDANIEL, speaker, social media influencer, host of the "Have You Heard?" podcast, and author of *You Are, All-Caps YOU*, and *Be Loved*

The enemy would love nothing more than to keep you hiding in shame, but Morgan is here to tell you what's true: that shame does not get the final say in your story. This is the book I wish I had as I wrestled with my past mistakes; one that reminded me how loved I was, and what it meant to live from a place of that love. Refreshingly honest, and coming from a girl who actually understands what it's like to struggle with regret, *Goodbye Hiding, Hello Freedom* is full of the tools and biblical truth we all need to be set free.

MEGHAN RYAN ASBURY, author of *You Are Not Behind*

MORGAN KRUEGER

goodbye hiding, hello freedom

TRADING YOUR SHAME FOR REDEMPTION IN JESUS

MOODY PUBLISHERS

CHICAGO

Edited by Ashleigh Slater
Interior design: Puckett Smartt
Cover design: Good Mood Design Co. / Riley Moody
Cover graphic of fig leaves copyright © 2024 by likorbut/Creative Market. All rights reserved.
Author photo: Annie Heath

Library of Congress Cataloging-in-Publication Data

Names: Krueger, Morgan, author.
Title: Goodbye hiding, hello freedom : trading your shame for redemption in
   Jesus / Morgan Krueger.
Description: Chicago : Moody Publishers, [2024] | Includes bibliographical
   references. | Summary: "Do you know what it's like to feel stuck in the
   cycle of shame? Through personal stories and biblical wisdom, Morgan
   offers encouragement to every soul who has ever felt disqualified from
   God's abundant life. Replace the burden of cultural lies with the truth
   of your freedom in Christ"-- Provided by publisher.
Identifiers: LCCN 2024006423 (print) | LCCN 2024006424 (ebook) | ISBN
   9780802432896 | ISBN 9780802471833 (ebook)
Subjects: LCSH: Shame--Religious aspects--Christianity. |
   Liberty--Religious aspects--Christianity. | Redemption--Religious
   aspects--Christianity.
Classification: LCC BT714 .K77 2024 (print) | LCC BT714 (ebook) | DDC
   241/.1--dc23/eng/20240329
LC record available at https://lccn.loc.gov/2024006423
LC ebook record available at https://lccn.loc.gov/2024006424

Originally delivered by fleets of horse-drawn wagons, the affordable paperbacks from D. L. Moody's publishing house resourced the church and served everyday people. Now, after more than 125 years of publishing and ministry, Moody Publishers' mission remains the same—even if our delivery systems have changed a bit. For more information on other books (and resources) created from a biblical perspective, go to www.moodypublishers.com or write to:

Moody Publishers
820 N. LaSalle Boulevard
Chicago, IL 60610

1 3 5 7 9 10 8 6 4 2

Printed in the United States of America

To Ryan Krueger,

This book, and my redemption story,
would have never been possible without you.

Thank you for always reaching for me. I ahava love you.

contents

PART 1

understanding
shame

and it went like this . . .

O n a normal Tuesday in late November of my sophomore year of high school, my dad sat me down and delivered a very surreal piece of news that would forever change my life: he had stage-four liver cancer.

I'll never forget where we were sitting, the feeling of the breath being knocked right out of me, and every step up the stairs to my room. I felt alone, scared, and abandoned.

What started as a diagnosis of a maximum of six months to live (that seemed far too short) became even shorter. This man who raised me, saw me, loved me, and called me his, quickly passed away less than two months later.

My teen years, which I thought would be marked by "finding myself and living it up," were now marred by total despair and loss. The months and years to come were consumed with questions I couldn't get answered, and I lived like a daughter abandoned by her earthly and heavenly Father.

But I hadn't always felt abandoned.

Years earlier, when I was a little girl, my dad loved to play a game with my sister and me that we liked to call the "bedtime game." Clever, right? The game was simple. My dad would tuck us into bed, turn off the lights, and walk out of the room, all the while keeping a grin on his face knowing what was about to happen.

Naturally, we would giggle the whole way through this portion of the game because we knew we were already plotting our plan of attack the second he walked out of the room. It was simple: sneak out of bed, turn on the lights, crawl on all fours (highly unnecessary, but it seemed important for the integrity of the game at the time) through our 1970s single-family ranch home into his office where he would pretend not to see or hear us creep our way toward him.

As we would get just inches away from him, as quick as the wind, he would spin around in his office swivel chair, scoop us up, and reverse attack us with tickles and giggles to no avail. This would continue for about five whole minutes (five minutes is a *lifetime* in tickle years), and then we would all three run it back.

Get tucked in. Plot our attack. Reverse tickle attack from Dad. Repeat. This would continue for a good ten rounds before my sister and I ran out of steam as we drifted off to sleep with heavy eyes and full hearts.

As I've gotten older, these memories have grown more and more dear to me. As much as I loved sneaking out of bed and finding my dad in his home office (oh, the thrill of the game), he must have loved it just as much, if not more. We, his daughters—whom he adored—wanted nothing more than to end our days getting wrapped up with him in games, tickles, and laughter. It must have brought him so much unceasing joy to know his children cared to move toward him with reckless and childlike abandon.

As a little girl, I sensed a similar draw toward God. I recall at a young age knowing and actually believing that God loved me. That He saw me. That He created me. And that nothing could separate me from that love. I don't know how, but back then, I didn't have a hard time simply believing it.

At the same time, I also remember being praised at my small Christian school for being able to articulate (more like regurgitate) spiritual truths at that same young age. Although these actions were seen as "good," they instilled in me a belief and permeated a lie that I could earn a little "extra" love from God. That He could "extra" approve of me. "Extra" see me. Be "extra" proud of how He created me because *look at me go*, quoting John 3:16 *and* Proverbs 3:5–6 in front of the whole school.

It was scary how good I got at giving people (and God) what I thought they wanted from me—all by the age of seven years old. The thing is, learning Scripture, being kind, and showing up for people are all good things, but when I believed the lie that they could earn me value, importance, or status, they became very, very harmful things. **This lie ushered in the one thing that separates us from God: sin.**

> The games I once played as a little girl with my dad were now replaced with a game of "hide and no seek" toward God. What I didn't realize is that everything I was looking for could be found in Him.

Somewhere along the way in this game of performance, I stopped running to my heavenly Father and started running in the opposite direction. The truth and lies got too jumbled, and I fed the monster of approval, affirmation, and acceptance I found in other places. If you've been there, stick with me.

The games I once played as a little girl with my dad were now replaced with a game of "hide and no seek" toward God. What I didn't realize is that everything I was looking for could be found in Him.

13

THE ORIGIN OF OUR IDENTITY

I love a good story. Who doesn't? After all, stories serve many purposes. It's how we get to know and relate with others and how we express ourselves. They also help us identify parts of our own story.

As cliché as it sounds, my favorite story growing up as a little girl raised in a small town in north Georgia was the iconic movie *Cinderella*. I was a sucker for it.

The charming and incredibly creative mice.

The duplicitous stepsisters.

The race against time.

The humility and timeless persona of Cinderella.

Prince Charming (enough said).

But there's one part of the story that always intrigued me the most: the dynamic of the glass slipper. (To the .000001 percent of you who have never seen *Cinderella*, spoiler alert.)

After every attempt of her stepsisters and stepmother to hold her back from attending the prince's ball created for him to find his true love, Cinderella is given one last chance by her fairy godmother to make a fashionably late arrival.

And with a "bibbidi-bobbidi-boo," Cinderella is provided with everything from a pumpkin carriage, a tailor-made gown (a true rags-to-riches story), and, of course, the famous glass slippers.

As the story goes, the prince falls in love instantly with Cinderella, but she leaves abruptly right before midnight, and he's left only with one glass slipper to identify her with. Despite her stepfamily's best efforts to inhibit Cinderella from true love, she is finally reunited with the prince by none other than, you guessed it, the glass slipper. The perfect fit of the slipper reveals that she is the one he had been looking for all along.

Before you write me off as a sappy romantic, the reason I love this story goes far beyond the narrative of a boy and girl falling in love.

And this definitely isn't a chapter or book about romantic relationships (even though you better believe we are going there in later chapters).

The reason it draws me in and whispers to a place deep in my heart is because it's the story of a young girl who once felt forgotten but now believed she belonged. It mirrors the reality that we have had belonging etched into the core of our existence since the beginning of time.

> We have had belonging etched into the core of our existence since the beginning of time.

Just like Cinderella's perfect fit, we fit into the creation story. We are not forgotten. This means that in God's economy, there is a place for you and me.

A place where we flourish.

A place where we feel no shame.

A place where we're able to receive forgiveness from others and ourselves.

A place where our past doesn't define us.

A place where we can be redeemed and made new.

A place of true and unlimited freedom.

A place our hearts long for. A place like Eden. But if you can even imagine, friend, a place even better than the garden. More on that later.

WHY ORDER MATTERS

As any decent storyteller knows, we can't fully know where we're going until we know where we've been. That's why the story of Adam and Eve in the garden of Eden is so essential for us to understand. Let's take a look.

(As you read, I encourage you not just to look to understand yourself in the narrative—there will be plenty of time for that. Look at what this text reveals about God first, then yourself.)

"In the beginning, God created the heavens and the earth. The earth was without form and void, and darkness was over the face of the deep. And the Spirit of God was hovering over the face of the waters" (Gen. 1:1–2).

Pause. Go back and read that one more time and really let it sink in. Then, let's continue.

The beginning. The origin of space, time, and existence. Before it all came to be, God was. He was there, putting everything into motion. See, God exists outside the borders of the world we live in. He is in it all, above it all, and before it all. He is the Great I Am, who was, is, and is to come (Ex. 3:14; Rev. 1:8).

We often project onto God the image we want Him to fit into. Simply put: we make Him small in our minds. We get uncomfortable thinking of a God we cannot fully grasp or make tangible this side of heaven. I've heard it cleverly put that just as God created us in His image, we tend to return the favor throughout our lives.[1]

If you're anything like me, it can be such a challenge as a finite human being to comprehend His infinite vastness and wonder. But as we are finite, God is infinite. As we find ourselves limited, God is limitless. As we are the created, He is the Creator. This is good news because this is the God who didn't stop at Genesis 1:2.

Then what did God do?

God created (in order): light (day), dark (night), waters, land, crops, moon, sun, and then living creatures (Gen. 1:3–25).

While He saw that all His creation was "good," up until this point, nothing had been made in the *imago Dei* (the image of God). It was all pleasing to God but didn't bear His image or imprint. But God still wasn't done.

"So God created man in his own image, in the image of God he created him; male and female he created them" (Gen. 1:27).

One thing that Moses, the author of Genesis, is helping us see here is that God is intentional. He is deliberate with what He makes, but He's also highly detailed in the order in which He creates. Order matters. I have a friend who loves to do puzzles. It calms her and helps her unwind after a long day. So naturally, when Christmas rolled around, I wanted to find her the perfect puzzle. After much searching, I found a beautiful vintage butterfly one that I couldn't wait to give her. Not only that, but I also was eager to see the final product.

You see, what I learned from my friend is that puzzling is an art. It takes intentionality and order. Any good puzzler knows that when starting a puzzle, you must put together the border first. It's simple: locate the pieces with straight edges and put them all together to create the framework, and only then can you make your way inward. And that's exactly what she did.

I know I'm biased, but let me tell you, the end result was such a beautiful formation of what was meant to be all along. A collage of some of the most beautiful and rare butterflies on earth. But without her intentional order or plan of action, beginning to end, the puzzle would have never been what it was supposed to be—finished.

Order matters. And if it matters that much with a puzzle, how much more did God put intention into His creation order?

Out of all creation, He created humankind last. Why do you think He did this? *Clearly, because He saved the best for last, Morgan.* Okay, while there's truth in that, there's a much better answer that reveals a depth about the heart of God toward us.

A PLACE OF BELONGING

I believe that one reason God created us last is because He wanted us to know from the very start that He, our *Abba*, goes before us in *all* things. What an invitation. To see God this way—as Abba—means in the

Greek to see Him as "Daddy." This is a God who longs for you and me to see Him in the most intimate form of a father and to cry out to Him, "Abba! Father!" (Rom. 8:15).

Like an Abba . . .

He didn't make us wait on an earth that was void.

He didn't make us stand in the darkness as He created light.

> It's who He is and who He will always be: *our true place of belonging.*

He didn't want to deprive us of the beauty of the seas, moon, stars, and the rest of His wonderful creation that points to His glory.

He didn't make us wait for our home to be prepared, but instead created us right in the middle of it.

I think that God wants us to know that what He did in Eden, He will do again and again and again: make a way for us. He will always prepare a place for us. A place of safety and belonging. He will always give light to the darkness for us. He will always whisper to us in our moments of doubt that we are not a misfit to Him.

With God, we will always have a seat at the table. What He did in the beginning is what He will continue to do throughout our entire lives. It's who He is and who He will always be: *our true place of belonging.*

We will never feel fully alive until we experience the depth of the warm embrace offered to us by our heavenly Father.

I'll never forget the safety and assurance I felt in my dad's arms when I was younger. My dad was a six-foot, lean-framed man with blue eyes that personified gentleness and purity of heart. He was lovely. His kindness shone on everyone, and he spent his adult life stewarding work well, loving his family, and investing in younger men who were seeking to follow God. I loved him so much and knew he undoubtedly loved me. No matter where he was, that's where I wanted to be. I didn't question how often, how deep, or for how long I could stay in his arms. Each night, I would stay right there, because where else would I go? I'd stay cuddled up with him, having no doubt that it was me who belonged there and no one else (except my sister, who was probably annoyed with me growing up for monopolizing so much of dad's lap—sorry, sis). When I was with him, I knew that I was safe. I was seen. I was home.

Isn't that exactly the pursuit of our heavenly Father toward us, but so much better? Doesn't the creation story this far show that God has extended an invitation for us to eternally abide in Him? To cry out to Him as Abba?

God has gone before us to show us He is safe. He is trustworthy. He isn't going anywhere. He doesn't just provide a home. He is our home. The God of Eden is the same God that is pursuing us right now through these pages. May our restless souls find rest in Him.

FULLY SEEN, FULLY LOVED

The other remarkable detail about humankind's creation narrative comes later in Genesis:

> The man gave names to all livestock and to the birds of the heavens and to every beast of the field. But for Adam there was not found a helper fit for him. So the Lord God caused a deep sleep to fall upon the man, and while he slept took one of his ribs and closed up its place with flesh. And the rib that the Lord God had taken from the man he made into a woman and brought her to the man. Then the man said,
>
> > "This at last is bone of my bones
> > and flesh of my flesh;
> > she shall be called Woman,
> > because she was taken out of Man."

Therefore, a man shall leave his father and his mother and hold fast to his wife, and they shall become one flesh. And the man and his wife were both naked and were not ashamed. (Gen. 2:20–25)

"There was not found a helper fit for him" (Gen. 2:20). So God does what He does best—He creates the perfect fit. He creates a partner and she is called "Woman." This is where you and I find our truest identity, friend. As one who fits. One who belongs. Just like a puzzle, the full picture wasn't revealed until the last bit was complete. Creation was good, but it wasn't in its fullness until God breathed life into the very last piece: woman. He created her last not out of forgetfulness, but that we might know that in Him, we "lack no good thing" (Ps. 34:10).

Many of us have lived years, maybe even decades, believing lies from the enemy that we are unwanted, unlovable, unvalued, and forgotten. Believing that we must live in shame over what we've done or what's been done to us. As you'll learn more throughout this book, this was my story for years. Because of brokenness from my past, I didn't know where I started and shame began. I would wake up in the middle of the night with flashbacks from the past and false narratives for my future. I found it impossible to live in the present because that meant coming to grips with the scars that marked my life, my relationships, and my view of myself (and my projection of how God must see me).

> Before we could do a thing, good or evil, **our identity was secured by** the one who calls us His beloved.

But our origin story from Scripture begs to differ. Before we could do a thing, good or evil, our identity was secured by the One who calls us His beloved. It wasn't until I came face to face with my true belovedness that God was able to do the work of redemption and reconciliation in my life. Only then did I get a glimpse of the truth laid out in Isaiah 61:7:

"Instead of your shame you will receive a double portion, and instead of disgrace you will rejoice in your inheritance. And so you will inherit a double portion in your land, and everlasting joy will be yours" (NIV).

Brennan Manning, on the topic of our belovedness, writes:

> God created us for union with himself: This is the original purpose of our lives. And God is defined as love (1 John 4:16). Living in awareness of our belovedness is the axis around which the Christian life revolves. Being the beloved is our identity, the core of our existence. It is not merely a lofty thought, an inspiring idea, or one name among many. It is the name by which God knows us and the way He relates to us.[2]

Don't you find comfort in the truth that there's nothing you can do to earn *or* sabotage your primary God-given identity? You are more loved, seen, purposed, valued, and secure in Him than you can even imagine.

As we move forward in this book together, let this reality be at the forefront of your heart and mind.

In the presence of your Creator, you can be like Adam and Eve in Eden: fully seen, fully loved, and free of shame. From the garden, we see that God is giving you and me a framework for a life of freedom that can actually be lived out today.

After years of wallowing in shame and hiding, *now freedom is my story*. And in these pages, you will see that it can be yours too. Not because of our righteousness, but because of the abundance of His goodness to call you His beloved who belongs.

As we all know, Eden didn't last, but our God's pursuit of us has never wavered.

So why don't we believe it? Why don't we live free? What's holding us back from a life of belief in our belonging?

And the story continues . . .

the origin of shame

When I started high school, my parents decided to take me out of Christian school and put me in public school. Up until this point, there were a lot of things I had never been exposed to. My whole life had been spent around people who wanted certain behavior from me: give the right answers, read your Bible, and live a moral life.

Within a matter of months, I went from one group of people who wanted certain things from me to a new culture that wanted completely different behavior from me: sneak out, go to the party, drink, and "hook up" with guys. And because I had become a master at giving others the version of me that I thought they wanted, it was just a matter of time before I fell into rebellion and turned my back against God. It seemed as though the years of learning the "right" answers and doing the "right" things became foreign to me almost overnight.

Recently at church, one of our teaching pastors posed a question to the congregation that really got my attention. He said, "So many people talk about what God's plan is for your life. But have you ever thought about, 'What is the enemy's plan for your life?'" And it's true. Just as much as God is writing a story for you that is better than you could ask or imagine, the enemy also has his pen and paper out to write a story contrary to the good plans of your heavenly Father. It's been the enemy's plan since the garden, and it's still his plan to this very day.

READY, SET, ATTACK

Something I have learned along the way is that there are two things Satan wants you and me to doubt: *the goodness of God and the danger of sin.*[1] He's made it his mission to instill these doubts in us throughout our lives.

The enemy first shows his hand with these two primary schemes in Genesis 3. Let's read:

> Now the serpent was more crafty than any other beast of the field that the LORD God had made.
>
> He said to the woman, "Did God actually say, 'You shall not eat of any tree in the garden'?" And the woman said to the serpent, "We may eat of the fruit of the trees in the garden, but God said, 'You shall not eat of the fruit of the tree that is in the midst of the garden, neither shall you touch it, lest you die.'" But the serpent said to the woman, "You will not surely die. For God knows that when you eat of it your eyes will be opened, and you will be like God, knowing good and evil." So when the woman saw that the tree was good for food, and that it was a delight to the eyes, and that the tree was to be desired to make one wise, she took of its fruit and ate, and she also gave some to her husband who was with her, and he ate. (Gen. 3:1–6)

Now this text alone has about as many moving parts as any given episode of *This Is Us.* So, let's take some time to unpack it.

Satan reveals to us here that he has three main areas of attack that cause us to doubt the goodness of God and the danger of sin.

Attack #1: Distorting God's Word

Do you notice how Satan casually strikes up a conversation with our girl Eve? He starts with a question. But not just any question—it's a question that is so close to the real thing but so far off from what was originally said to Adam by God. "Did God actually say, 'You shall not eat of any tree in the garden'?" (Gen. 3:1). The serpent knew good and well that this statement was not what God had spoken over them. God gave Adam clear instruction that he was to enjoy and eat of every tree in the garden, "but of the tree of the knowledge of good and evil you shall not eat, for in the day that you eat of it you shall surely die" (Gen. 2:17).

Right then and there, Satan ushered in confusion by taking God's positive command and distorting it to sound like the real thing—but with a negative spin.

Listen up: if the enemy cannot get you to easily sin, he will always use the tactic of distortion. It's often said that the greatest lie the enemy uses is the one that's one degree off from the truth. Chills (not the good kind).

Distortion always leads to confusion, questioning, and temptation. Satan will take a command by God that leads to *flourishing* (example: *Enjoy the good things in the garden I've set before you and live in freedom*) and make it sound like *withholding* (example: *Why wouldn't God want you to be happy and have what looks appealing to you? He must not want you to be free!*). Because the reality is that the Tree of the Knowledge of Good and Evil can serve as a reminder that we're not God, and that's a really good thing. This is not a tactic to withhold, but to allow us to live in freedom as His beloved children who can come to Him in all dependence and neediness.

Satan is a master of distortion (John 8:44). He mainly does this by taking statements from the Word of God, ones that even sound familiar to us, and twisting them to appeal to our selfish desires.

As I drifted farther and farther from God starting in high school, the familiar whispers of "Did God actually say?" became louder and louder in my mind.

Did God actually say don't sleep with your boyfriend? But you love him. Doesn't God want you to be happy?

Did God actually say don't get drunk with your friends? But you come alive when you have a few drinks! Doesn't God want you to be fully yourself?

Did God actually say honor your father and mother? Your parents just don't get it. If they did, then they'd let you do what you want to do.

Did God actually say turn from your sin and He would forgive you? He probably wouldn't forgive you anyway at this point. Just stay here with me and I'll show you the way to your own truth.

In order to fight the distortion and the lies of the enemy, there is only one defense: you and I have to know God's voice. Knowing His voice is the only way not to be fooled when we are tempted to reach out to lesser loves.

To put it another way: we fight lies by knowing truth.

Theologians speculate that one of the reasons the serpent went for Eve before Adam is because Eve hadn't heard the command to not eat of the tree directly from God, so instead she was relying on secondhand information.[2] When we don't hear something from the source itself, we become vulnerable to attack.

We fight lies by knowing truth.

Think of someone right now whom you love, and who loves you. Imagine if, for your whole life, you had someone else telling you for that person that they love you. After a while, wouldn't that truth be almost nearly impossible to believe? Wouldn't doubt creep in that maybe you're not loved? God did not intend for us to receive His truth and love secondhand. He has made a way for us to know and hear from Him firsthand through His Word.

Scripture is laced with the only thing that can allow us to fight lesser loves: love itself.

For me, a lot of my faith was secondhand. Although I had seeds planted when I was younger on the "Christian walk," I relied more on people telling me how to follow Jesus than actually cultivating a relationship with Him. Over time, because I depended on other sources more than the source Himself, when met with the temptation to go my own way over God's way, I had no line of defense. I was vulnerable. And I drifted.

We have access to the source that allows us to fight the attacks of the enemy. Because of Jesus, we don't have to rely on secondhand information. We can intimately and personally know the Father, who withholds no good thing from His children.

Attack #2: Convincing Us to Entertain a Conversation with Him

Have you ever been in a casual conversation with someone that seemed so innocent, and then all of a sudden it took a negative turn? Maybe it was the moment someone's name got brought up, or when someone said, "If I tell you this, you promise you won't tell anyone?" Or maybe you simply just got that nervous, sweaty feeling knowing you probably shouldn't be in that conversation. The trickiest part is that sometimes it's even with our best friends and people we do life with.

If we're capable of dangerous conversations with those we love and trust, how much more should we be on our guard in conversation with those we don't know? Those whose character or integrity we know nothing about?

In Genesis 3, I have to give it to Satan. After all, the biggest descriptor we have of him here is the word "crafty" (Gen. 3:1). So, it shouldn't come as a surprise that his plan was to lure Eve into an "open discussion."

He asks a pretty enticing question, one that Eve even felt like she could explain: "Did God actually say, 'You shall not eat of any tree in the garden'?" (Gen. 3:1). How tempting to take the bait.

Here's a rule of thumb for sticky conversations like this one: just because you have an answer, doesn't mean you should always give it.

Sometimes saying nothing is the wisest thing you can do if you find yourself in a dangerous conversation. Proverbs 17:28 speaks to this: "Even a fool who keeps silent is considered wise; when he closes his lips, he is deemed intelligent."

We see this example in the earthly life of Jesus. Time and time again, Jesus knew His audience and was able to discern who to enter into true conversation with. He knew whether someone was asking questions from a pure place of wanting truth or was seeking to entrap Him. Jesus' moment with Pilate right before His death sentence is a powerful example of wisdom in silence:

> Now Jesus stood before the governor, and the governor asked him, "Are you the King of the Jews?" Jesus said, "You have said so." But when he was accused by the chief priests and elders, he gave no answer. Then Pilate said to him, "Do you not hear how many things they testify against you?" But he gave him no answer, not even to a single charge, so that the governor was greatly amazed. (Matt. 27:11–14)

We see here that even at the highest peak of accusation in Jesus' life, when He could have had a million rebuttals, comebacks, and "stick it to the man" moments, He responded with silence.

Discernment on how and when to respond to the lies of the enemy is key. Sometimes it's with silence, but other times it's not. Discernment comes when we know truth and seek wisdom from the Holy Spirit in those tough moments. When being tested in the wilderness, Jesus gives us a framework for when silence isn't enough and we do need to respond to dangerous conversations:

The tempter came to him and said, "If you are the Son of God, tell these stones to become bread."

Jesus answered, "It is written: 'Man shall not live on bread alone, but on every word that comes from the mouth of God.'"

Then the devil took him to the holy city and had him stand on the highest point of the temple. "If you are the Son of God," he said, "throw yourself down. For it is written:

"'He will command his angels concerning you,
>   and they will lift you up in their hands,
>   so that you will not strike your foot against a stone.'"

Jesus answered him, "It is also written: 'Do not put the Lord your God to the test.'"

Again, the devil took him to a very high mountain and showed him all the kingdoms of the world and their splendor. "All this I will give you," he said, "if you will bow down and worship me."

Jesus said to him, "Away from me, Satan! For it is written: 'Worship the Lord your God, and serve him only.'"

Then the devil left him, and angels came and attended him." (Matt. 4:3–11 NIV)

So how did Jesus respond? With unarguable truth that He knew firsthand from Scripture. He read it. He meditated on it. He abided in it. And He fought with it. Jesus considered it the ultimate form of truth, and with every "It is written," He shut down the conversation. As believers, this passage shows us that we are called to respond to the enemy at times, but never to hear him out.

> Jesus considered Scripture **the ultimate form of truth**, and with every "It is written," He shut down the conversation.

When all else fails, may we fight like Jesus with the battle cry, "In the name of Jesus, get away from me, Satan, the master of lies. I worship and serve God and God only."

These are our fighting words. Let's be women who have the discernment to know when to fight with holy silence and when to respond with firsthand knowledge of God's truth.

Attack #3: Appealing to Our Greatest Distorted Desire—to Be Like God

I think that the mystery of God and His ways makes us more uncomfortable than we're willing to admit. There are things on earth that we find ourselves unable to reconcile about why God does what He does and it can lead us to extreme sadness, confusion, despair, frustration, and anger. It breaks a part of our hearts that we feel can't be mended.

Like when a loved one dies.

Or when disaster strikes.

Or when a relationship becomes broken.

Or when you feel unlovable.

Or when you lose the dream job.

Or when after years of trying and praying, you still haven't conceived.

Or when forgiveness from God, others, and yourself feels too far out of reach.

In uncertain times, we're prone to doubt God rather than to trust in Him to do more than we could ever ask or imagine. Whether you have at this point in your life or not, we will inevitably all face trials of many kinds that can cause us to doubt God.

Problem is, when we doubt God, we start to try and put ourselves in the place of God. With a small view of God, we look at our life's situations and think, *How do You not see what I see, God? If You were really good and all powerful, You wouldn't have let this happen.* And what do we do? We try to take matters into our own hands. We stop leaning on the God who cares and is working out a plan greater than we can see at the moment, and we assume the position in our lives as ultimate judge. But as I learned, we make really crappy gods.

John Mark Comer, in his book *Garden City*, puts it like this:

> I would argue the desire to be great was put there by the Creator himself. After all, we're made in his image.
>
> The problem is this desire, which in its embryonic, innocent state is so, so right, is quickly warped and soiled and bent out of shape by the ego.
>
> We devolve from a desire to be great to a desire to be *thought of* as great.
>
> From a desire to serve the weak to desire to be served *by* the weak.
>
> From a desire to save the world to a desire to *have* it.[3]

If you were to ask me in high school and college (at the peak of my rebellion against God) if my lifestyle and sin were rooted in a distorted desire to be God, I would have laughed (and maybe cried a little inside) as I walked away perplexed and low-key offended. I would have told you that, of course, I don't want to be God. I never could, and I would never try. But looking back, this was the root of every decision I made that led me to drift farther and farther from the Father I once loved in my younger years.

The enemy started to do what he does best in our seasons of brokenness and vulnerability, which is to try and convince us that God is not good, He is not for us, and He has left us. As a fifteen-year-old that missed her daddy and couldn't imagine how a God who loved her could take away such a good one like mine, I took the bait. I felt completely alone and did the only thing I knew to do: I made myself my own god.

I resonated with the internal struggle Eve must have faced that day in the garden that changed her whole life:

But the serpent said to the woman, "You will not surely die. For God knows that when you eat of it your eyes will be opened, *and you will be like God*, knowing good and evil." So when the woman saw that the tree was good for food, and that it was a delight to the eyes, and that the tree was to be desired to make one wise, she took of its fruit and ate. (Gen. 3:4–6, emphasis added)

Satan knows that if he can get us to doubt God's inherent goodness, we will always try to take matters into our own hands. But the pursuit to be equal with God is always a hollow one. It's the impossible task that will forever leave us empty, seeking, and unanchored.

This is at the core of all sin—the desire to be God. We want to rule, reign, and control our lives. We want to write the story. We want the ink and paper. The postmodern age shows us this. We cling to phrases like "Live your own truth" and "You control your destiny" and "You do you." We want the throne. We want the glory. But glory was never meant to be ours.

I know this has been heavy, so let me offer you the good news: we're not God, we can never be God, and that's a really good thing. Even in our rebellion, God is still on the throne, and has not left you or me. Just like my story, you are not an abandoned child. You still have a heavenly Father who loves you, no matter what you've done or what's been done to you.

It doesn't matter your scorecard because God is not a scorekeeper. He's a good Father. He just wants His daughter to know that even in your game of hide and no seek, He will still find you. Thomas Merton puts it beautifully when he says, "Quit keeping score altogether and surrender ourselves with all our sinfulness to God who sees neither the score nor the scorekeeper but only his child redeemed by Christ."[4]

No matter where you are right now or what your past looks like, believe the truth that your sin doesn't disqualify you from a life of freedom, but is the very place that God begins His pursuit to win you back. It's in that state that Paul proclaims, "God shows his love for us in that while we were still sinners, Christ died for us" (Rom. 5:8).

If that resonates with your soul, take heart, friend. In this chapter, we have accomplished a very good thing: we have learned the attacks of the enemy that cause rebellion against God. And we have been reminded that in our walk with Jesus, we are given the invitation to walk right back to Him without hesitation.

> Your sin doesn't disqualify you from a life of freedom, but is **the very place that God begins His pursuit** to win you back.

But, as we just learned, the enemy uses his attacks to present a different kind of invitation to us. This invitation we're about to look at is what I like to call "the second most powerful force on earth." And it's the very reason I wrote this book.

the second most powerful force on earth

You're such a hypocrite, Morgan. All the things that you said you stood for, you have thrown out the window. How could you do that? Hurt your friends, give yourself away, be so selfish? Good luck trying to have God, someone else, or even yourself love you after all you've done."

This was spoken to me at the young age of seventeen by a "close friend" from my hometown. Can you believe someone actually said that to me? Even as I write it out, it's shocking. She is the kind of person that, deep down, I know doesn't have my best interest at heart, is more interested in manipulating me than actually knowing me, and doesn't believe in grace or the power of redemption.

From the start, I really never trusted this person, but the sharpness of those words stuck with me. Not just stuck with me. They marked me. Broke me. Changed me.

Because words matter—both the words spoken to us by others and ourselves. Words carry the power of life and death.

James, the brother of Jesus, sums up the power that our words carry:

If we put bits into the mouths of horses so that they obey us, we guide their whole bodies as well. Look at the ships also: though they are so large and are driven by strong winds, they are guided by a very small rudder wherever the will of the pilot directs. So also the tongue is a small member, yet it boasts of great things.

How great a forest is set ablaze by such a small fire! And the tongue is a fire, a world of unrighteousness. The tongue is set among our members, staining the whole body, setting on fire the entire course of life, and set on fire by hell. For every kind of beast and bird, of reptile and sea creature, can be tamed and has been tamed by mankind, but no human being can tame the tongue. It is a restless evil, full of deadly poison. With it we bless our Lord and Father, and with it we curse people who are made in the likeness of God. From the same mouth come blessing and cursing. My brothers, these things ought not to be so. (James 3:3–10)

As much as I wish I could say that was the only time this happened with this particular friend, it wasn't. The "small fires" James talks about grew and grew and seemed impossible to put out. You know those people that seem to follow you everywhere? It's like, come on—of all people, really, *this* friend? This girl had to go to the same college as me and continue to say hurtful things to me. This person had to take note of every new place I was going, every effort I made to escape my past, and follow me there.

I'm sure you're thinking, *How can one person have such a grip over your life? After all, it's only one opinion.* The reality is, even amidst dozens of voices of truth, having someone in my life that was a loud competing voice of lies still impacted me. With every friend that reminded me that I am forgiven and loved, this one voice felt like she had the final say. But the key word is *felt*.

36

WHAT IS SHAME?

Oftentimes, our feelings can lie to us. Amen? Our feelings are a gift from God, but they aren't always trustworthy. They can spew lies that we're worthless, inadequate, unlovable, incapable, or incompetent instead of the truth that we are loved, forgiven, valued, and created for a purpose. When we don't take control over our thought life, false feelings arise.

I love the way Jennie Allen describes our thought life: "One God-honoring thought has the potential to change the trajectory of both history and eternity. Just as one uninterrupted lie in my head has the potential to bring about unimaginable destruction in the world around me."[1]

We must learn to take our thoughts captive in the fight against lies and shame. The apostle Paul gives us the perfect framework for what and how to think: "Finally, brothers, whatever is true, whatever is honorable, whatever is just, whatever is pure, whatever is lovely, whatever is commendable, if there is any excellence, if there is anything worthy of praise, think about these things" (Phil. 4:8).

Back to my friend (for lack of a better word). Over the years, this destructive friend who spoke lies over me eventually caused a massive buildup of shame.

Okay, let's get to the million-dollar question: What is shame?

> Shame doesn't just say you've made a mistake, **it says that you are your mistakes.** It's a lie attacking your truest identity.

A definition of *shame* that I came across and deeply resonate with explains it as "a self-conscious emotion arising from the sense that something is fundamentally wrong about oneself."[2]

Unlike guilt, which focuses on what you've done, shame goes deeper and focuses on *who you are*. Shame doesn't just say you've made a mistake; it says that you *are* your mistakes. It's a lie attacking your truest identity. How do I know this? Because it's from the enemy, the master of lies. You can always know the validity of something based on where it comes from.

The enemy tries to convince us of lies by using forms of the truth— and that's where it gets tricky.

The truth is, I gave the enemy a lot of ammunition through the years to use as flaming darts against me in his pursuit of wanting me to live under a blanket of shame. I did run from the God I once loved and dove headfirst into a life of rebellion against Him. I did betray friends. I did lie to cover up sin. I did manipulate guys out of my need for control. I did treat my body in a way that wasn't honoring to myself or the One who created me. And I did live a life that was outside of His good design for me. Those things were very, very true about me. The enemy used these truths to convince me I should live a life of shame.

After my dad passed away, I was like a textbook case of "daddy issues." Feeling alone, abandoned, and fatherless, I ran to temporary comforts to fill a void that only Jesus could fill. But instead of these worldly comforts filling me as they falsely promised, they emptied me.

Emptied me of my identity.

Emptied me of my purity.

Emptied me of my worth and value.

Emptied me of memories from nights I don't remember.

Emptied me of my belief that I could ever have a chance at a godly marriage one day.

Emptied me of . . . me.

So when faced with an evaluation of myself, I had nothing to reference or hold on to except for the things I had thrown away. At that time, my belief was: How could I feel anything *but* shame after all I had done?

LOVE VERSUS SHAME

To understand *why* this happened, let's pick back up with our new (but very, very old) besties Adam and Eve right after they ate the fruit from the forbidden tree. As the story goes: "Then the eyes of both were opened, and they knew that they were naked. And they sewed fig leaves together and made themselves loincloths" (Gen. 3:7).

Friend, do not mistake this act of hiding as a fashion statement. The symbolism seen through the context of shame brings actual tears to my eyes and a pit in my stomach.

Up until this point in all of creation (we're only three chapters into the beginning of time, but still, you get the point), there had been no separation from God. That means *zero hiding, zero covering up, zero shame*.

This act of hiding and covering themselves was an entirely new thing. This is so foreign to us today because clothes are a fundamental part of our everyday lives (I hope), but in the garden of Eden, they just weren't. They weren't because Adam and Eve knew that they were created in the image of God and it was a beautiful thing for the Creator to behold His perfect creation. No one told Adam and Eve to do what they did. It was pure instinct to cover their bodies directly following this act of disobedience.

I want you to hear this loud and clear: **if love is the most powerful force on earth, shame is the second.**

Just as Mexican food and tight jeans just don't go together, love and shame will never mix. The thing that makes shame so dangerous is that it pulls us away from the God who loves us.

Love pulls us toward God when we've blown it. Shame pulls us away.

Love is laced with grace for ourselves and others. Shame's rope has zero slack for extending grace.

Love tells us that we're covered. Shame tells us to take cover.

Love summons us to come out of hiding. Shame demands hiding for fear of being exposed.

Shame lies. Shame comes to rob us of our true identity. Shame tells us to take hold of another cup than the cup of our double portion. Shame tells us that our inheritance isn't as beautiful as promised by our heavenly Father (Isa. 61:7). Shame tells us that we should take matters into our own hands. Shame covers up and scatters our lives into a million little pieces. And that is what it did for me. I let the shame of my past steal so much from me. On certain days it felt too strong to bear. Shame brought back memories that I would have done anything to forget.

> If love is the most powerful force on earth, shame is the second.

All of this came to a head in 2019. When I think of that year, I think of my battle with shame. Looking back, I can't believe a whole year can be consumed by one big lie.

SHAME SCATTERS, JESUS GATHERS

Now it's important to note that by 2019, I had been walking with Jesus personally for about five solid years. I had seen Jesus redeem and do so much in my heart and life. I was (and still am) in an incredibly happy marriage with my favorite person on planet earth. And I was even working in my all-time favorite ministry job encouraging young women to surrender their lives to Jesus and to live in freedom.

On the outside, it looked like I was thriving. It appeared that I was "past the past," if you will. You would think that surely by that point in my walk with Jesus I was no longer gripped with shame and was now joyfully living in the truth found in 2 Corinthians 5:17: "Therefore, if anyone is in Christ, the new creation has come: The old has gone, the new is here!" (NIV).

But on the inside, the shame was all-consuming. So much so that memories from my past started to infiltrate my thoughts as I lay in bed at night. My dreams had become flashbacks from past regrets. Even my first thoughts in the morning were laced with anxiety from things I had done.

Shame was like a sleeping lion at the end of my bed that I thought would devour me at any moment by the slightest attempt to outrun it.

But like I said, it wasn't until 2019 that I was hit with the reality of how much I had let shame define me.

It's hard to sum up why shame had become so real for me that year. Shame can be caused by such a combination of factors. For me, there were three defining factors or moments that year that made it impossible to suppress the shame I had carried for so long.

First, it marked ten years without my dad. That meant ten years of fighting abandonment, feelings of unworthiness, and fatherlessness. It was a mile marker in my life that made the things I had been walking through a lot more real to me and a lot harder to suppress.

Also, in the spring of that year, we had joined a new community group that we were really excited about. It was a combination of our real-life friends and acquaintances from church that we knew would be great to have in a group. It was a group that I knew were safe people, but also people that knew how to challenge each other. It didn't hurt that we also had a lot of fun together.

One night at small group, one of the couples had us over to sit in their dreamy backyard under the string lights and around a bonfire. If you know me, you know this is my love language.

Conversation started out casual and light that night, but at some point it took a turn. To be honest, I couldn't even tell you what I was saying (probably because the context of it had become so second nature to me), but someone in our group turned to me and said, "Morgan, I have never in my life met someone who is as hard on themselves as you are."

Ouch. Something about that statement knocked the wind out of me. It had nothing to do with who said it because, knowing them, I know they said it with purity of heart and as someone who cared, but it still stung. It was a combination of embarrassment and the fact that "the truth hurts." I did my best to play it off and somehow diverted the conversation away from myself for the rest of the night.

I went home that night perplexed and filled with questions. I respected this person and valued their opinion. So it forced me to face the question: Are they right? Turns out, they were. I had so normalized self-deprecating thoughts and language that I was blind to it. I was so covered in the fig leaves of shame that I started to think it was a good look for me.

Another big part of shame surfacing that year was that because of the season of weddings and babies, I found myself taking a lot of trips back to my hometown in Georgia, a place that housed so many of my ex-boyfriends and memories that I hoped to never revisit. Above all, it was a place that I ran into that old friend almost every time I went home.

I'd like to take a mini detour here to address the topic of returning home. I've spoken to a lot of Jesus-loving women through the years who share this struggle to return to their hometown. Our hometown can represent so much for us who have had radical life change once we left. It can represent hurts, regrets, loss, old versions of ourselves, and of course, shame. It can house people who haven't seen all that Jesus has done to radically rescue and redeem.

Around this time, I just dreaded going home. But God showed me something that year that I started to believe for maybe the first time in my life: **Shame wants to take us back to our past to relive it. Jesus wants to take us back to our past to redeem it.**

In the midst of the fight with the memories and that one friend from my past, I knew deep down there was something else that had the power to cover me. Just as one voice had such a grip of lies on me, there was (and is) One that had a stronger grip of freedom and redemption laid out for me (and for you).

God knew what the fig leaves meant that day in the garden. The day that sin entered the narrative is the same day that God started His eternal pursuit to win us back to Himself: "And the LORD God made for Adam and for his wife garments of skins and clothed them" (Gen. 3:21).

> Shame wants to take us back to our past to relive it. Jesus wants to take us back to our past to redeem it.

Did you catch that? God made garments of skin and *clothed them*. This implies that He sacrificed and slaughtered an animal for His children in order to give them a better covering. If this isn't foreshadowing, I don't know what is. Since the beginning of time, God was setting up the narrative for Jesus, the perfect sacrifice, to come, die, and trade our pitiful fig leaves for an eternal covering. This is where freedom is found.

Shame scatters, Jesus gathers.

A BETTER COVERING

If what you're reading right now resonates with you, please know you're not alone in this moment. The truth is, I still have that friend in my life that occasionally tries to make their way back to resurface my past, making me feel so hidden in fig leaves that I can't tell where the shame ends and I begin.

In the winter of 2019, I was exhausted and weighed down by the shame that I couldn't seem to cast off. I went to a Bible study taught by one of my mentors one night. She was laying out the concept of time and God's plan for the fullness of it. I came alone, sat down in my chair, looked up, and you won't believe it . . . *the friend was there.* I couldn't make this stuff up if I tried.

I felt so anxious the whole time knowing she was in the room and fought back tears at the thought that she would call me out for the phony that I believed I was.

At the end, my mentor asked everyone in the class to write out this question: *God, how do You see me?*

In the moment, I didn't write anything. I didn't because I couldn't. The minute I wrote that question on my paper, I sensed so clearly that the word God was pouring out on me was "proud."

This word *terrified* me. Proud? *There's no way*, I thought—and I had a person in the room who would agree with me. So, I sat there, fighting back tears, looking for the closest exit and some fig leaves laying around, just in case.

I actually left that night writing nothing in that space.

Amidst all the fighting voices, I sat down the next day (with tears in my eyes and hope in my heart) choosing the better portion and good cup of truth (Ps. 16:5). With that, I want to make a confession to you.

The friend who has followed me everywhere is me. But it's actually not me, it's shame. It's rooted in lies from the enemy (remember, he's real). And those lies from him had been around for so long it almost felt like a part of me, but it's not who I am. I made a choice that day to not allow that voice in my life anymore.

To be honest, I still have days when I doubt, but I made the choice to take hold of the truth that I'm covered by forgiving grace. I decided that day to not let shame have the final word. It had been too long, and I was done.

If you are weary, worn, and shame-filled, I want to invite you into the same journey that God has taken me on. One that trades shame for joy, regret for redemption, and fig leaves for freedom.

Since 2019, I have been convinced of this truth: God will redeem as many shame-filled moments, memories, spaces, relationships, and regrets as you will let Him.

His better covering provided through Jesus pleads with you and says, "Come to me, all you who are weary and burdened, and I will give you rest. Take my yoke upon you and learn from me, for I am gentle and humble in heart, and you will find rest for your souls. For my yoke is easy and my burden is light" (Matt. 11:28–30 NIV).

> God will redeem as many **shame-filled moments, memories, spaces, relationships, and regrets** as you will let Him.

He will move into even the darkest moments of your life and continue the work He began all the way back in the garden. When He took away the sad fig leaves that Adam and Eve clung to and clothed them that day, He was pointing to a future covering that He would provide in Jesus—one that offers true freedom and rest.

EVERY AREA MEANS EVERY AREA

Fast forward to present day, Jesus is still redeeming parts of my life and past.

Get this: right now, I am wrapping up this chapter at a coffee shop in my hometown, the one place that represented my shame and hiding for so long.

When prepping for this book, I mapped out my chapters months before I actually started writing. I picked my date for when the writing would start, and I felt called to write one chapter a week. Little did I know the week I'm writing this chapter on shame is the one week God was taking me home for a trip I've had planned for months. If that's not the redeeming hand of a good heavenly Father, I don't know what is. At the right time, He will redeem every area of our lives that we allow Him to.

Not only am I here, but God took me a completely different route as I was heading into town yesterday. I found myself on a route I normally never take and one that isn't even the fastest way home. Confused on how I ended up on that back road, I sensed the spirit of God reminding me: *every area means every area.*

This particular route led me by two places that I try my best to avoid while I'm home: my high school and my dad's grave—which happen to conveniently be located on the same street. For the first time (maybe ever) since I graduated, I drove by my high school and actually began to smile. I felt peace. I felt gratitude. I decided to let the past point me to how far God had brought me. And then what did I do? *I looked forward,* both literally and spiritually.

Then came the graveyard. I pulled in. I walked around and prayed. Maybe for the first time, in the middle of a place that represented death for so long, I celebrated the life I've been given in Christ. Every area means every area.

Friend, what's that area for you? What space are you still grasping at the fig leaves of guilt and shame and trying your best to cover up? So many of us have salvation, but we are still holding on to places we refuse to surrender. But when we dare to be forgiven, freedom follows. As Brennan Manning says, "When we dare to live as forgiven men and women, we join the wounded healers and draw closer to Jesus."[3]

We have been given full freedom in Christ, but it doesn't guarantee we walk in it. Just like a gift, freedom through Jesus is being offered to you. It's waiting for you to reach out your hand and take hold of it in your own life. Will you take it?

Lastly, how does God see you? *He's proud.* Because of what Jesus has done, you have the opportunity to live redeemed, made new, forgiven, and free. I invite you through the truth in His Word to take on your true identity once and for all—a daughter who makes her Father proud. Not because of what you've done, but because of who calls you His.

This truly is the beautiful inheritance—trading fig leaves for freedom.

PART 2

sources
of shame

dealing with fatherhood wounds

S omething that most people don't know about me from the outside is that I love basketball. And let me be clear, I love watching it. Playing? Not so much. I do have the fondest memories playing it as a little girl and having my dad coach my team, but I could never quite figure out how to throw up a decent shot as a leftie. We all have our strengths, I guess. And to be honest, there were many years where I didn't care much to watch the sport. But it all changed when I met Ryan Krueger. Ryan isn't just a fan of the sport. He is a super fan. He has a genuine love of the game and it's something I (have learned to) love about him, even if it means our dates revolve around his home team's schedule (Go Mavs!).

Each spring, the Krueger household gears up for all the March Madness fun. We make our brackets, I act like I know what I'm doing while Ryan actually does, and we soak up the action of it all. If you are a basketball fan, you know that the 2024 Women's March Madness Tournament had a breakout star: Caitlin Clark. Although her team, the Hawkeyes, lost to South Carolina 87–75 in the championship game, Clark became the NCAA's all-time leading scorer and is already making her mark on women's sports and sports as a whole. So much so that she became the first pick in the 2024 WNBA draft.

It shouldn't surprise you that Caitlin's athletic ability and competitive nature runs in the family. In fact, her dad (who was also her coach as a little girl) played college basketball and earned First Team All-Conference honors and Second Team All-Conference for basketball.

"I see a lot of myself at times in Caitlin in terms of her passion for the game," her father shared. "All in all, that's really what drives her and makes her the player that she is."[1]

In God's good design, He models for us on earth what it means to reflect our fathers. God in His goodness gives us gifts, talents, passions, and even mannerisms that point to the reality that *we came from somewhere*. We each bear a father's image. Feeling grateful in that moment for that truth, I started to think on my own story in relation to my earthly father.

My dad was a lot of things. He was kind. He was loving. He was patient. He was softhearted (a total crier). He was intentional. He was introverted. But one interesting fact about my dad is that he had a deep passion for writing. He was gifted in his words and actually wrote and published three books in his lifetime. In his last book, *The Crimson Ride* (a five hundred-plus page book on the history of Alabama football—yeah, he was a big fan), he recalls a difficult season and a turning point for him:

> The first thing I did after I was let go from my job was to take a whole week off. I wanted some time to think and to ask myself what exactly I wanted to do in my career. One of the dream scenarios was I wanted to write. I had no idea on how or what I wanted to write about, I just wanted to do something in that vein. Now the question was what I should write.[2]

He goes on to share about the process of writing his first book, a short comedy on those who were considered the "bottom half" of society. (Fun fact: you can look it up on Amazon and they have just one new copy available for the reasonable price of $974.83. Any takers?)

This first book, published two days before I was born (another fun fact), unfortunately didn't launch my dad into a successful career as an established writer, but what it did do is give his daughter, me, a launchpad and a true love for the power of the written word.

My dad was writing on the side for most of my childhood. I got to see the struggles, the joys, the hard days, and the days of breakthrough. If I could talk to my dad today, thanking him for passing on this passion and gift of his would be at the top of my list.

> God in His goodness gives us **gifts, talents, passions, and even mannerisms** that point to the reality that we came from somewhere.

And now, here I am years later, writing my very first book right around the age that he started writing his. What a joy to reflect my father's image.

THE FATHERHOOD FIG LEAF

At the same time, the topic of my earthly dad has also caused a lot of pain and hurt. It has brought me panic attacks, deep wounds, depression, and believe it or not, shame. I carried a "fatherhood fig leaf" around for years before I could even identify what it was that made me so fearful, guarded, and broken.

As you know, my dad got suddenly sick when I was fifteen with stage-four liver cancer and was given six months to live, but ended up only having not even two months.

I watched as the chemo failed.

I watched as he grew thin and frail.

I watched as he struggled to stay awake.

I watched as he drifted away.

I watched the dad I once knew now have nothing to give.

The night before he passed away, I rushed to the hospice center after school to hopefully have one more moment with him. One final hug and, "I love you. You were a really great dad." But I was met with my greatest fear: he had entered into a coma and it wasn't likely he would return to me.

I sat by his bed for hours as loved ones came in and out to visit and pray. I never left his side. I held his hands in mine, realizing in that moment we had the exact same hands. One more way God allowed me to bear his image. (Don't worry, his hands were long and skinny. I don't have man hands). And I tried to imagine saying goodbye to this man I loved so deeply. This man who had raised me. The man who had given me a love for Jesus, ping-pong, people, and of course, writing. That night, I said my last one-sided goodbye.

After this huge loss in my life, the days, months, and years that went on without him were paralleled with my beliefs about God.

My dad had abandoned me. Therefore, God had abandoned me.

My dad couldn't stick around for me. Therefore, God couldn't stick around for me.

My dad didn't know how much I loved him. Therefore, God must not think I loved Him either. That's probably why He left me.

Probably one of the most unexpected struggles in all of this was the shame that the loss of my dad brought on. When I met someone I didn't know or who didn't know my story, I feared the question, "So, what does your dad do?" The thought of trying to disclose or fumble over the fact that my dad was dead brought on so much shame and embarrassment.

There were even times when I lied about him being gone. I never knew why this was, but the shame of not having a dad felt all too real.

Friend, I know that everyone's story is different. Some people have had incredible dads, and some, like me, had great dads that we've lost. And some of you have had fathers that have hurt you in unimaginable ways. Maybe you've been left, abused, neglected, or just plain hurt. Everyone's stories are unique to them, but the enemy is not that creative when it comes to his attacks against those who have fatherhood wounds. He will convince us that we are abandoned daughters any chance he gets. He knows that if we can feel abandoned by our earthly dad, it's impossible not to open the door of temptation to believe our God has left us.

This leads me to another fig leaf that has stuck to so many of us since we were little children that we might not even know exists. And that's our relationship with our earthly father and the connection this relationship has to our Abba, our heavenly Father.

WHERE FREEDOM BEGINS

Whether you realize it or not, the relationship you have or don't have with your father on earth can have the power to either bind your heart to God for a lifetime or make you question His goodness.

The reality is, so many of us have wounds from broken relationships with our earthly dads, and we can't help but project their image and the painful experiences we had with them onto God. I know for some, this specific topic of fatherhood is a really hard road to walk back down, but it is imperative that we go there if we want to live a life of true freedom. *Freedom starts with a correct view of God.* If that view is severed, we will find ourselves with walls, broken hearts, and abandonment issues that won't give God a chance to show Himself for the good, perfect Father that He is.

A. W. Tozer reminds us of this importance when he starts off his book *The Knowledge of the Holy* with this statement: "What comes into our minds when we think about God is the most important thing about us."[3]

> Freedom starts with a **correct view** of God.

So let me ask you, what do you think about when you think of God? No, really. Take a moment, grab a pen and paper, and write out the very first thoughts that you think of when you ponder God. Is He near or distant? Is He loving or wrathful? Father or judge? Is He compassionate or apathetic toward you? Until we become honest with ourselves about our true thoughts toward God, the fig leaves stay.

The beautiful part in the journey of discovering God is that when we learn about Him, we also learn our true identity in the process. When we know God, we know ourselves. This is the only way to true knowledge of self: knowledge of God. I love how Jen Wilkin puts it: "Fullness of joy results when we seek to reflect our Maker. It is what we were created to do. It is the very will of God for our lives."[4]

Reflecting someone else can feel like both a blessing and a curse when it comes to our earthly father, but it's in that space that God wants to shatter the simple, human standards we attempt to reflect onto Him. Even if we've had the best dad in the world, God is still better.

So who is God?

Pastor Dane Ortlund gives us a list of characteristics of God that can we can cling to when we're tempted to see Him incorrectly:

- He is the God of intimacy (Gal. 4:6).
- He is the God who deeply cares for us (Matt. 6:25–34).
- He is the God who hears our prayers (Matt. 7:7–11).
- He is the God who lovingly disciplines us for our good and our growth (Heb. 12:3–11).

- He is the God who forgives us when we've blown it (Luke 15:11–32).[5]

He's the Dad we've always wanted but didn't know we could have. And He allows us to bear His likeness out of an abundance of His goodness.

Jonathan Edwards, author of *Left*, whose father walked out on him when he was young, shares his story:

> Growing up, I was so scared of my dad and so confused by his leaving. As this continued to eat away at my heart, I began to have the same questions about God. I was scared of him. I was hesitant to talk to him or ask him for things because I thought he'd get mad. I thought God would find a reason to leave me too. I thought God wouldn't love me for who I was.[6]

I'm not going to lie; it took me a long time to start to really see and trust God as Father. Even today, I have to go back to the truth that I am indeed taken care of and not abandoned by God. Some days are easier than others, but I find that when I think of God as Father, I also return to my truest identity as daughter.

How did I begin to step out of hiding and see and call God by His true name, Abba? By knowing God's true essence, called the "attributes of God." The attributes of God helped me identify and clear the weeds of the misconceptions I had about God—and they can do the same for you. There are so many attributes that we could look at, but in the next chapter we are going to look at three attributes of God that prove that, unlike our earthly fathers, God is a perfect Father.

dealing with God wounds

One of my favorite pool games growing up was the penny game. I know my parents loved it as well because—not joking—this game would keep me and my sister occupied for *hours* in the summer. Basically, we would bring a handful of pennies to the pool, throw them in, and race to see how many pennies we could find. Whoever found the most pennies won the game.

Competitive by nature, I wanted to win probably more than I cared to admit. There was one problem: my stubborn self *refused* to wear goggles, giving my sister an obvious advantage over me. As much as I desired to win and find all the pennies, without the proper eyewear, I would just drift around picking up any blurry speck I could find.

Eventually, my sister stopped wanting to play with me because it was a blowout every time. Without the proper equipment for the game, my vision would always be impaired, impacting my ability to see clearly and participate well.

But the penny game isn't the only area of life where seeing well matters. As we talked about in the last chapter, we need a clear view of God to start to let Him into our lives to love us, care for us, and redeem us as His daughters. So in this chapter, we are going to cover just three attributes that scratch the surface of beginning to see who He really is. We are going to look at God's goodness, God's immanence, and God's love.

A. W. Tozer clearly explains these qualities, or *attributes* of God as things about God that are not only true, but also ones that we can know because He has revealed them to us:

> An attribute, as we can know it, is a mental concept, an intellectual response to God's self-revelation. It is an answer to a question, the reply God makes to our interrogation concerning Himself.
>
> What is God like? What kind of God is He? How may we expect Him to act toward us and toward all created things? Such questions are not merely academic. They touch the far-in reaches of the human spirit, and their answers affect life and character and destiny.[1]

With that, let's look at God's goodness, God's immanence, and God's love.

GOD'S GOODNESS

If I'm being honest, I almost veered away from this attribute of God because something about it at first glimpse seems oddly underwhelming. In today's age, the concept of "good" has lost a bit of the wonder and meaning it deserves.

The word *good* can be so relative in our language today.

"How was the pizza?" *So good.*

"I'm finally starting to live my own truth." *Well, good for you!*

"How are you?" *I'm good, just busy.*

But this core, intrinsic attribute of God is absolutely crucial to seeing Him as just not God, but as the Father that He is. Psalm 145:9 proclaims, "The LORD is good to all, and His tender mercies are over all His works" (NKJV).

Growing up, I had a love for chocolate chip cookies. I still do! But when I was little, I had no gauge or care for self-control when it came to how many I wanted to eat. When I thought of what was "good," my mind went straight to that soft-baked Chips-Ahoy! peel-back cookie package.

In those days, it was a constant battle between my dad and me at the end of dinner on how many cookies I was allowed to have. I would scream and cry, and one night, in a moment of complete cookie desperation, I yelled out in front of my whole family, *"Don't you love me?"*

I couldn't wrap my cookie-crazed mind around how a good dad wouldn't give his daughter what she truly wanted: soft, chewy, chocolatey goodness.

Some nights I would get one. Some nights I would get two if I was lucky. But some nights, I wouldn't get any cookies, especially if I threw a fit and dramatically questioned my dad's love for me.

What would start as a conversation about cookies would turn into a whole verbal brawl where I would get sent to my room as I cried over my internal frustration of not being given what I wanted, when I wanted it.

Years later, I understand now what my dad was doing: he was being a good dad who put what was actually best for his daughter ahead of giving me what I wanted that might not be best for me. Sometimes we have similar responses toward God. When we have unmet expectations, unanswered prayers, or a skewed meaning for the word "good," we tend to miss the beauty of who our good Father is.

> When we have unmet expectations, unanswered prayers, or a skewed meaning for the word "good," **we tend to miss the beauty** of who our good Father is.

He is the Father who knows how to give good gifts, and every good and perfect gift is from Him (James 1:17).

He is the Father who makes all things work together for the good of those who love Him (Rom. 8:28).

He is the Father who sees you as "very good" (Gen. 1:31).

I have found in my own life that I have a tendency to assign the title of "good" to things that serve me. Advice that is easy to follow without internal change: good. The plans that perfectly go my way: good. Even the Scripture that doesn't make me uncomfortable: good. But God's goodness is so much deeper and better. It's a goodness that knows better, cares deeper, and sees what's absolute best for us even when we don't. A goodness that says, "'For my thoughts are not your thoughts, neither are your ways my ways,' declares the LORD. 'As the heavens are higher than the earth, so are my ways higher than your ways and my thoughts than your thoughts'" (Isa. 55:8–9 NIV).

I don't know about you, but I'll take this version of good any day. A good that never fades, never changes, and never disappoints. A good that won't just give me what I want in that moment, but sees beyond the moment and has good, eternal gifts laid out for me. A good that isn't just based on what He does, but who He is.

The goodness of God is a covering and safe haven for those who dare to walk into it. Dare to step out of the confines of the way you see what's good and look beyond to the glorious goodness of a perfect Father.

GOD'S IMMANENCE

This is a big one, especially for those of us who have experienced abandonment or distant fathers.

When we say that God is immanent, it means that He is a Father who is near and involved in the inner workings and details of our lives, our relationships, and our desires. He isn't a God who simply created us and then stepped away to let the chips fall where they may. No, God is Immanuel, the One who is with us (Matt. 1:23). He is near to the brokenhearted (Ps. 34:18). He is compassionate toward the weary. He invites those with heavy burdens to come to Him and abide with Him. He is the God of the great invitation (Matt. 11:28–30).

This is best seen through the sending of His Son, Jesus. The reality is, God had every reason to keep His distance from us. He is a holy God (another attribute I encourage you to study), and we are a broken people. There was nothing we could do to make our way back to Him on our own. And being our Father, He knows that. So the immanent God took action. He sent His one and only Son to earth to put on flesh to dwell among us. The apostle Paul tells us that, "He is not far from any one of us. 'For in Him we live and move and have our being'" (Acts 17:27–28 NIV).

To be completely vulnerable with you, because of the death of my father, this is by far the hardest attribute for me to trust and lean into.

When we lose a father or when a father leaves, we sometimes do strange things as part of the grieving process. Things we hesitate to tell people because they go against all logic or reason and are just plain strange. If you have one of these strange things you did, I hope you find a friend in me in this moment. It can't be stranger than mine.

For years after my dad's passing, I would every so often call my dad's phone number. I knew I wouldn't get a response. I knew it would just ring and ring and ring. But I did it anyway. (404) 597-7279. Over and over and over.

Like I said, strange. I knew that I wouldn't get the result I desired. A scenario in which he would pick up the phone on the third ring and tell me about the long trip he had taken and how he can't wait to get back to me. It was never going to happen. But I did it anyway.

It was nearly impossible for me to not project the inevitable distance I experienced from my dad onto God. After a while, I stopped dialing God too. I stopped giving God the opportunity to answer, an answer that would have been on the first ring.

But just because I spent years not calling on God, it didn't change the fact that He was and is immanent. Close by. Near.

Friend, if you've struggled with this like I have, the same is true for you. Your Father is closer than the very air you are breathing right now. He desperately wants you to invite Him into every area of your life in order to give you freedom, redemption, and hope. In fact, there's nowhere you can go to escape His immanent outpouring.

> Our God meets us on **the lightest path or the darkest alley.** Tell Him what you need.

I love the cry of David as he proclaims this attribute of God:

> Where shall I go from your Spirit?
> Or where shall I flee from your presence?
> If I ascend to heaven, you are there!
> If I make my bed in Sheol, you are there!
> If I take the wings of the morning
> and dwell in the uttermost parts of the sea,
> even there your hand shall lead me,
> and your right hand shall hold me.
> If I say, "Surely the darkness shall cover me,
> and the light about me be night,"
> even the darkness is not dark to you;
> the night is bright as the day,
> for darkness is as light with you. (Ps. 139:7–12)

Our God meets us on the lightest path or the darkest alley. Call on the immanent God. Tell Him what you need. I promise you He will always pick up when you call.

GOD'S LOVE

Much like the word *good*, *love* is another word we often neglect and misuse. I don't know about you, but I've actually had my heart broken by people who said they really loved me. I've been manipulated in the name of "love" and I have been given every reason to see love for everything it is not. In a sense, love has been dragged through the mud at times in my life. My guess is that in one way or another, you can relate. That is why it is absolutely crucial that we understand what it means when we say God is the root and the essence of the true version of love.

One of the greatest metaphors in all of Scripture for the Father's love is found in Luke 15. In short, a father has two sons. One son demands his inheritance. He runs away, uses it, and squanders everything he's been given. Ashamed and downcast, he musters up enough courage to return home and try and convince his dad to at least let him back into the home, even if as a servant. Let's pick up at the moment of his return:

> But while he was still a long way off, his father saw him and felt compassion, and ran and embraced him and kissed him. And the son said to him, "Father, I have sinned against heaven and before you, I am no longer worthy to be called your son." But the father said to his servants, "Bring quickly the best robe, and put it on him, and put a ring on his hand, and shoes on his feet. And bring the fattened calf and kill it, and let us eat and celebrate. For this my son was dead, and is alive again; he was lost, and is found." And they began to celebrate. (Luke 15:20–24)

So many people read this and focus only on the prodigal son. But this story is about so much more. A major theme in it is the father and how he demonstrates God's love.

Biblical scholars explain that in those days, the father would have been wearing a long, heavy robe with multiple layers. Not only that, but it was seen as disgraceful for a man of status to run like we see in this parable. But this father wasn't just any father. He was one who had abundant grace and love toward those who were his own. He deeply desired his son to return, even if the son didn't believe his father wanted him to. *This is love.*

When we read this story and focus on the father's role in it, it's imperative we look at the end of the story when his older brother finds out the younger brother has returned.

> He was angry and refused to go in. His father came out and entreated him, but he answered his father, "Look, these many years I have served you, and I never disobeyed your command, yet you never gave me a young goat, that I might celebrate with my friends. But when this son of yours came, who has devoured your property with prostitutes, you killed the fattened calf for him!" And he said to him, "Son, you are always with me, and all that is mine is yours. It was fitting to celebrate and be glad, for this your brother was dead, and is alive; he was lost, and is found." (Luke 15:28–32)

What does this show us about God the Father's love?

God's love is not contingent on what we do or don't do. How little or how much we "blow it." God's love knows no limits and will never run out on us. It is inexhaustible. For the son who returned home full of shame and regret, everything the father had was his. For the son who never departed from him, everything the father had was also his. This is the Father's love—filled with reckless abandon for those He calls His own. He is ready to trade your shame for His abundant love. A love that cries, "though my father and mother forsake me, the LORD will receive me" (Ps. 27:10 NIV).

After my dad died, there was a shame that haunted me. At fifteen, I had no idea how to watch someone I love die or how to even be around him. I found myself being completely emotionally shut off toward him out of a place of deep sadness and fear of losing him. On top of all that, because I wasn't able to make it to him in time before he went into a coma, I never got to tell him how much I loved him and that he was a good dad.

With him gone, the daunting reality that I would never get to tell him these truths caused pain in the deepest parts of my being. To the point where I didn't know if I would be able to live the rest of my life knowing that I had blown it in his last days. The enemy attacked me hard with this lie and I lived every day in despair and regret.

About a month went by as I walked in this specific pain. One morning around that time, I woke up and found myself physically unable to get out of bed. The grief was attacking every part of my body and I had no strength to go on another day. My mom allowed me to stay home that day from school and I quickly drifted back to sleep. I woke up around noon, figured I should try and get up and eat something, and stumbled to the door. I opened the door, looked down, and saw a letter sealed with an envelope with my name on it. I immediately recognized the handwriting—my dad's. Unknown to me that he even wrote me a letter, I was met with nerves, excitement, and fear. *What will he say? Will he be disappointed in me as a daughter over how I handled the months leading up to his death?* I made my way downstairs and slowly opened the letter and braced myself for whatever it might say.

The letter read: "Morgan, if you are reading this, I have died and am now in Heaven with God." What followed shook me to my core:

> God's love for us will never be contingent on our performance or perfection.

I want you to know that I know how much you truly loved me.

Did I read that right? I read it again. And again. And again. Did he really just say that he knew how much I loved him? What I was expecting was for him to say that he loved me. But he knew I already knew that. What he somehow knew was what I would truly struggle with: the fear of him not knowing my love for him. In that moment, chains broke. God freed me from the one lie that I would have believed for the rest of my life.

A lie that could have broken me.

A lie that could have made me take my life.

A lie that would have held me back from freedom.

Every area means every area.

That day, just like the prodigal son and the older brother, I learned that God's love for us will never be contingent on our performance or perfection. It was in our inability to perform or be perfect that Christ died for us, offering us a way out of our manmade fig leaves. As Tozer encouraged, "His love is an incomprehensibly vast, bottomless, shoreless sea before which we kneel in joyful silence and from which the loftiest eloquence retreats confused and abashed."[2]

As we can see through God's love, He is ready to redeem fatherhood for you when you're ready. I have heard it said that salvation is free, but surrender is costly. Will you surrender even the darkest places to the Father who is eager to pour out His goodness, immanence, and love onto you as His beloved?

All you have to do is allow the Father to love you and respond with loving Him back. As eighteenth-century German poet Gerhard Tersteegen beautifully articulates in his timeless hymn "The Blessed Journey," when we learn to be loved, everything else will follow:

Let Him lead thee blindfold onwards,
　　Love needs not to know;

Children whom the Father leadeth
Ask not where they go.
Though the path be all unknown,
Over moors and mountains lone.[3]

As I think back to that nostalgic summertime pool game, I like to think of those pennies as attributes of God. All around us, clear for us to see, and ready for discovering if we have the proper equipment. But instead of goggles, God pours out His Word, His Spirit, and His Son—all helping us to see the truth that He is good, He is near, and He is full of love.

dealing with dating wounds

H i, I'm Ryan." *Oh, well, hello, Ryan.* I stared up at the tall, dark, and handsome man looking down at me in the lobby of a Chicago hotel. What first struck me about him were his kind eyes and excitement for life.

Ryan and I met when we were placed on the same team to go spend a year in East Asia and share the gospel with college students. Both having come from the University of Alabama, I was shocked that we had never met each other before, but I was glad to be meeting him at that moment.

Just as soon as I was hopeful that there might be a spark there, doubts and shame began to creep in.

If Ryan only knew my past . . .

I'm sure Ryan only dates a certain type of girl . . .

I've blown my chances with true, godly guys like Ryan . . .

(SPOILER ALERT!) Fast forward to today, Ryan and I have been happily married for years. Now, I wish the story was that simple, but that's not the case. There was a lot that happened between that day in the hotel lobby and our wedding day. A lot. Because as we discovered in the last chapter, salvation is free, but surrender is costly. This is true of fatherhood and also incredibly true of the role relationships play in our life and our freedom.

GOD'S GOOD DESIGN FOR RELATIONSHIPS

Up until I met Ryan, I can honestly say I had never been in a relationship with a guy who truly walked with Jesus intimately. To give you a better picture (and to hopefully relate), here are some of the guys I had dated in the past:

- The Passive Type: "I don't want to do anything that you're not comfortable with."
- The Half-In Type: "I don't have a church home, but if you want me to come with you I will."
- The Jealous Type: "Who is that guy? I feel like he was hitting on you. Are you into him?"
- The Steamroller Type: "I told you it was up to you how far we went physically, so that's on you."
- The Good Type: "I don't believe in God, but I totally respect your beliefs."

To sum it up, the guys I had dated in the past were not godly men. They hadn't been transformed by the gospel, therefore not sold out for Jesus. Whether you are single or married, maybe you can relate to my dating history. Perhaps yours is similar. And as much as it's easy to play the victim and say that I was mistreated by the men I dated, I think we as women need to own our part as well. When it comes to who we date, we have a choice. The choice (while so much easier said than done) is simple:

- Option 1: Settle
- Option 2: Take God's good design for relationships seriously

If you're anything like me, God's good design for relationships was not spoken of growing up. Instead, I was given a rigid list of "don't dos" when it came to dating, sex, and relationships.

Don't do anything immoral.

Don't do anything Jesus wouldn't do. (Jesus never had a relationship—so this one was a real head scratcher for me.)

Don't kiss boys. (They're cute though . . . so why?!)

Don't take your clothes off.

> Without an accurate outline of the way our soul flourishes under the guidelines our Father God has set for us, I prepared my fig leaves for inevitable use.

Definitely *don't* have sex. (If you ever watch the movie *Mean Girls* with a group of people, you will realize that it is often Christians who laugh the hardest at the line, "Don't have sex, you'll get pregnant and die."[1] In all its absurdity, it's what so many of us actually heard growing up).

Instead of being shown the beauty in how and why God's good design is what it is, I was simply told "NO" to all the things that, ultimately, my flesh wanted. And without an accurate outline of the way our soul flourishes under the guidelines our Father has set for us, I prepared my fig leaves for inevitable use.

So, what *is* God's good design?

God models for us in the garden in Genesis 2 and tells us in other places in Scripture the way He intended for relationships to be. One man and one woman, becoming one flesh under the covenant of marriage.

A marriage built on sacrifice, trust, and centered on the redeeming power of Jesus Christ.

A marriage that is covenantal. Unlike a contract that can be broken when one side fails to meet the requirements, a covenant represents an unbreakable commitment to love. An "I'm not going anywhere, no

> God-breathed marriage is sacred, **modeling the extravagant love** that Jesus poured out for us on the cross.

matter what" kind of love.

A marriage built on promise and duty, not just emotions and passion.

One of the clearest passages in all of Scripture that talks about God's good design for marriage is found in Ephesians 5:

> Submit to one another out of reverence for Christ.
>
> Wives, submit yourselves to your own husbands as you do to the Lord. For the husband is the head of the wife as Christ is the head of the church, his body, of which he is the Savior. Now as the church submits to Christ, so also wives should submit to their husbands in everything.
>
> Husbands, love your wives, just as Christ loved the church and gave himself up for her to make her holy, cleansing her by the washing with water through the word, and to present her to himself as a radiant church, without stain or wrinkle or any other blemish, but holy and blameless. (Eph. 5:21–27 NIV)

God-breathed marriage is sacred, modeling the extravagant love that Jesus poured out for us on the cross.

But the relationships I had leading up to meeting Ryan looked nothing like that. I knew they would never lead to the flourishing and pure love that I so longed for. I stayed in that cycle for years until finally I fell in love.

FALLING IN LOVE

But, here's the plot twist. I did not fall in love with Ryan—that wasn't going to be for a few years. No, I fell (back) in love with my first love—Jesus.

What changed it all for me is when I realized I would never know what to look for in a relationship until I was willing to look to Jesus. I had to fix my gaze on Him before I could ever gaze upon another and see him as God sees him. I knew I would never be the wife my future husband deserved until I sat and learned who first calls me His beloved. The satisfaction I had been looking for in guys would never be met until I let my soul be filled by the only One who can satisfy.

Along with that, I needed space and time to heal from my sexual past. Sexual shame was one of the biggest hurdles that I faced when it came to true movement forward with Jesus. I felt broken. I felt scattered. I felt unlovable. I felt used up. I felt like I had disqualified myself from a good future when it came to the type of guy I actually wanted to be with.

As we've learned, the enemy attacks in areas where he takes a part of the truth and tries to make it the *whole* truth.

For example, when it came to my relationships, I was walking away from God's good design. I *was* settling. I *was* giving myself away when I knew better. I *was* grasping for temporary pleasures instead of trusting that the best things are meant to be enjoyed within marriage. All of that was true and I needed to take that seriously. But what Satan tries to do is say that because of our decisions, we are no longer qualified for a life and marriage that truly pleases the heart of God.

While I dated a lot of different types of guys, I tended to end up with the "good" guys a lot. Time and time again, it was the habit I couldn't break. I would meet a "good" guy, we would pretend like the feeble boundaries we set would keep us from crossing the line, and then we would cross it. And if I can just be a little too relatable here, in the moments of temptation, I believed the lie, which was distorted from truth, that I'd already done it once and blown it. So, what difference did it make to do it again? Clearly a rhetorical question here, because if I had actually asked myself (or God) the question, I would have heard the truth found in 1 John 1:9 ringing in my ears: "If we confess our sins, he is faithful and just and will forgive us our sins and purify us from all unrighteousness" (NIV).

What Jesus was offering was forgiveness and true purification every single time. But for years, I didn't take Him at His word. So the "good" guys would come, and the "good" guys would go, and with each relationship, I felt less and less myself and more and more filled with shame.

I use the phrase "good" guy here because there is a very real distinction I had to realize when it came to the type of guys I would let into my life. There is a *huge* difference between a "good" guy and a "godly" guy. I can't tell you how many college girls I've talked to who have told me, "But Morgan, he's suchhhh a good guy." If I had a nickel for every time I heard that, I would be a millionaire.

> "Good" guys will leave you unsatisfied, unled, and unengaged from the heart of God.

Yes, there are lots of "good" guys out there, but "good" guys just don't cut it when it comes to what you're looking for in a future spouse. Now, I'm guessing that if you're married and reading this, you know what I'm talking about—either because you made this discovery before or after marriage. (If it's after and you married the "good" guy, can I encourage you to give your relationship to God and ask Him to do what only He can do in your husband and marriage. God can transform your "good" guy into a godly one.) So, let me take a few minutes to talk to our single friends.

"Good" guys will leave you unsatisfied, unled, and unengaged from the heart of God. So, if you are single and reading, let me ask you to think about a few things.

Do you want someone created in the image of God? Yes, that can be a "good" guy.

Do you want someone to remind you that *you* are created in the image of God? Only a godly guy can do that.

Do you want someone who respects your boundaries? A "good" guy might be able to sustain that for a while.

Do you long for someone to actually be the one to set the boundaries? That will only come from a godly guy.

Do you want someone who will attend church with you because he wants to make you happy? That has a "good" guy written all over it.

Do you want someone who will be plugged into a local church and has godly men pouring into him? That's your godly guy.

A "good" guy thinks he's good, but a godly guy knows he's not. A godly guy knows he's a sinner in need of grace and that's why he needs Jesus.

This sounds so harsh, but the enemy loves "good" guys. This is because they look so close to the real thing that we are longing for, but ultimately, they're counterfeit to a guy who truly knows and loves Jesus and will lead you as you should be led.

Sometimes, our biggest stumbling block is the "good" guy—and I am speaking from experience. My most toxic relationship and the one that held me back from fully surrendering to Jesus for years was a "good" guy. He cared about me, wanted good things for me, would even go to church with me, and called himself a "Christian," but his life was not bearing fruit. And, while I know it takes two to fall into temptation, he definitely did not lead me when it came to purity. It was no time at all before we took it too far.

And it's not that he didn't mean well. "Good" guys can mean well. But ultimately, apart from Christ, a "good" guy will never be able to see you through the lens that, as a believer, is your primary and most important identity: daughter of the King. I got to the point in my life and dating patterns with "good" guys that I began to realize that this was an empty pursuit. Without the mind and heart transformed by

Christ, a "good" guy will never be able to see you and love you as you are deemed worthy to be seen.

Single friends, don't settle for the "good" guy.

BOUNDARIES

I can't go on without addressing the elephant in the room—and that's the question:

How far is too far?

It's a question that if you're single, you may be asking yourself right now. But it's also one that those of you who are married might be haunted by as you look back at your dating past.

Before we can truly answer this question, we have to identify the first problem: the question itself. When we ask, "How far is too far?" we are asking for someone or something to restrict us and constrain us so we don't go too far. But just like a big red button that says, "Do not push," the broken human condition is prone to reach out and take what isn't meant for us. Until we have a greater love and reason why, we'll never just obey a set of guidelines.

When I was younger, I was naturally pretty selfish. My little self had this mentality of "I'm going to get me mine." (By the way, whoever wants to argue that humans are born good, just go to any department store and watch moms and their children in the toy aisle.) So my dad decided to test out this theory of how we handle boundaries.

One day when I was younger, my dad came home with two huge, soft-baked cookies from a local bakery. (Yes, a lot of my stories contain food. I clearly have a weakness for cookies. Welcome to my life.) I could barely contain myself. I was so excited and, like a good dad, he didn't withhold from me and gave me one of the cookies. It was everything I hoped it could be—perfectly soft, the chocolate was still gooey, and it just melted in my mouth! It was one of those cookies that halfway through you start to get sad about the reality of it being gone. I know I'm not the only one who experiences this.

Quickly after it was gone, my eyes went right to the other cookie still in the bag. My dad explained to me that he had picked that one out for my sister, but because she wasn't home yet, he told me that he would give me a bite of her cookie. But just one. One bite and then it goes back in the bag. That was the deal.

I can still remember it. Him handing me the cookie. Me holding it in both hands ready to attack. I'm not proud of what came next. Knowing that I had one bite and one bite only, I opened my mouth, brought the cookie near, and took the *biggest* bite my tiny little mouth could hold. Naturally, my dad, who should have disciplined me, just laughed knowing that his theory was proven right.

> Without a greater love, we will never stay **within the boundaries God has set** before us. We will always try to take hold of things that aren't meant for us.

This silly story had heavier spiritual implications when it comes to how far is too far. His theory, which he would explain to me later, was this: *Without a greater love, we will never stay within the boundaries God has set before us. We will always try to take hold of things that aren't meant for us.* Unfortunately, this valuable lesson was lost on me in my years of navigating physical boundaries.

Without a primary love for Jesus, we will never have any reason to save ourselves for what sex is meant to be inside of God's good design for marriage. And if we are married and we aren't first satisfied in Christ, there could be a temptation to seek comfort outside of our marital boundaries. Just like the cookie, we may try to take matters into our own hands and grab hold of what we think we want in that moment without any vision for the future that awaits us when we wait on God.

So, let's reframe the question. Because in order to get the better answers, we have to be willing to ask the better questions. Instead of "How far is too far?" let's posture our hearts to seek out the truth of, "What is God's good design with sexual intimacy?" It's a question for all of us—single or married.

A LOVE STORY FOR THE BOOKS

Song of Solomon 4 is going to be our landing place for the greatest picture of God's plan for us as we think and live out our romantic relationships.

This passage, a declaration by Solomon (the groom) to his bride, gets a little steamy, so just be prepared. (And people say the Bible is boring . . . please.)

Let's start in verse 7:

You are altogether beautiful, my love;
　　there is no flaw in you.
Come with me from Lebanon, my bride;
　　come with me from Lebanon.
Depart from the peak of Amana,
　　from the peak of Senir and Hermon,
from the dens of lions,
　　from the mountains of leopards.

You have captivated my heart, my sister, my bride;
　　you have captivated my heart with one glance of your eyes,
　　with one jewel of your necklace.
How beautiful is your love, my sister, my bride!
　　How much better is your love than wine,
　　and the fragrance of your oils than any spice!

Your lips drip nectar, my bride;
> honey and milk are under your tongue;
>> the fragrance of your garments is like the fragrance of Lebanon.

A garden locked is my sister, my bride,
> a spring locked, a fountain sealed.

Your shoots are an orchard of pomegranates
> with all choicest fruits,
> henna with nard,

nard with saffron, calamus and cinnamon,
> with all trees of frankincense,

myrrh and aloes,
> with all choice spices—

a garden fountain, a well of living water,
> and flowing streams from Lebanon.

Awake, O north wind,
> and come, O south wind!

Blow upon my garden,
> let its spices flow. (Song 4:7–16)

The bride responds, "Let my beloved come to his garden, and eat its choicest fruits" (Song 4:16).

The groom chimes in once more with, let's just say, an undeniable confidence that he came, he saw, and he conquered: "I came to my garden, my sister, my bride, I gathered my myrrh with my spice, I ate my honeycomb with my honey, I drank my wine with my milk" (Song 5:1). If that's not a good design, I don't know what is.

No hiding, no hesitation, no questioning.

What we have here is one man, one woman, and one love, entering into wholehearted enjoyment of one another. No hiding, no hesitation, no questioning. Not that there is a formula within sexual intimacy, but we do see a pattern that we can cling to and put great hope in within the gift of marriage.

The groom sees his bride as she ought to be seen and pursues her out of that place.

"You are altogether beautiful" (Song 4:7). He is captivated.

"How beautiful is your love, my sister, my bride!" (Song 4:10). He acknowledges her true identity.

"Awake, O north wind, and come, O south wind! Blow upon my garden, let its spices flow" (Song 4:16). He calls upon her and invites her in.

The bride then reciprocates her love and gives her groom full access to her body, her love, and her affection.

"Let my beloved come to his garden" (Song 4:16). Permission is granted.

". . . and eat its choicest fruits" (Song 4:16). She gives her best to him. Unashamed and free.

The groom confirms his enjoyment of her.

"I came to my garden, my sister, my bride, I gathered my myrrh with my spice . . ." (Song 5:1). He did what he said he was going to do with love and gentleness.

"I ate my honeycomb with my honey, I drank my wine with my milk" (Song 5:1). I'll let this one speak for itself.

Friends, if you're single and longing for the gift of marriage, there is no space for the question, "How far is too far?" when we look at this beautiful expression of intimacy between this husband and wife. They were experiencing each other for the first time, full of holiness, expectancy, and freedom. And, if you're married and wish you could go back and change things from the past, take it from me, *redemption is possible.* There's nothing you've done that is too big for the cross. Jesus died for your past. Jesus rose for you to see redemption and freedom in your marriage.

THE GIFT OF INTIMACY

Let me put it like this. Think of sex, intimacy, and physical closeness as a gift. A really, really good gift. But it comes in one of those boxes that many of us have been given at some point in our lives. You know, one of those huge boxes that you open and look inside of only to realize there's another wrapped gift in it. Then, once you open that box, you find box after box after box. As the boxes get smaller, you finally reach the center to find one little tiny, precious box. Your heart is pounding with excitement as this is *finally* what you've been waiting for.

What is inside?

It's a key. It's beautiful and shining in a way you've never seen, and it only unlocks one room, as any special key would. This key makes you want to share it and the opening of that room with someone special.

In that moment, you realize that it's not *just* the key and the opening of the room that you want to share with one special person. You understand that the huge box and all the boxes inside of it were meant to be unwrapped with that same person the entire time.

That's how it is with sex. It's not just about the act of sex. It's about every sexual and intimate experience God has given us to be "unwrapped" inside of marriage. Every "gift" you unwrap before its proper time is one less gift to be unwrapped inside God's design for intimacy in marriage.

And when you open even the outer boxes with someone who isn't your husband, the key becomes confusing. You start to question what room it's even meant to unlock. You look around and realize you don't even remember the first time you started unwrapping the gift as a whole and the key becomes less and less precious. The key that's meant to represent the unlocking of a good gift now represents confusion and disordered desires.

Matt Chandler, in his incredible book on marriage *The Mingling of Souls*, explains: "If he gives you a gift, he wants you to enjoy it as it is designed to be enjoyed, which will ultimately lead to your satisfaction—not only with the gift itself but also with himself as the Giver."[2]

Why is sex so precious? Because it was created by God, therefore it is holy. It is sacred, created to be an expression of pure, sacrificial love. I know it sounds weird, but the love and desire God has for us, His children, is immeasurably stronger than even the most passionate sex. He longs for us. He has given us this symbol of sexual intimacy, not just for our own pleasure and satisfaction, but as a reminder of His desire to have holy union with us.

> There is no past, whether it's something you've done or something that's been done to you, that isn't **covered by the blood of Jesus** on the cross.

What a beautiful design!

There are so many of us out there who have unwrapped our gift before its proper time. That was me. And if that's you, please know that there's hope.

Jesus came to earth to redeem all things, even our broken sexual pasts. There is no past, whether it's something you've done or something that's been done to you, that isn't covered by the blood of Jesus on the cross.

Remember our saying: every area means every area.

WHAT'S BROKEN CANNOT FIX ITSELF

If you desire for Jesus to redeem your past, He will. And not just that, He's actually eager and excited to do so. The prophet Isaiah assures us of this: "Come now, let us reason together, says the LORD: though your sins are like scarlet, they shall be as white as snow; though they are red like crimson, they shall become like wool" (Isa. 1:18).

He is the only One who has the power to take you from broken to whole. From scarlet to snow. Just like the bride of Solomon, you can walk down the aisle knowing that you are made pure and that under Christ, "there is no flaw in you" (Song 4:7).

But friend, whether it's sexual purity or some other area in your life, white-knuckling your way to morality will never cut it.

I cannot tell you how many times I told myself, "Stop it. Stop making the same mistakes. Stop giving yourself away. Quit it and be better." My success rate playing that game was 0 percent. I feared I would never turn from sexual impurity and that I would subsequently have to settle for one of those "good" guys at best.

Trying to be "enough" in our own strength will never cut it. Until we see ourselves as broken people who don't claim our own "enoughness," we will keep returning time and time again to the destructive behaviors that rip open good gifts before their proper time. We must hold tight to the sufficiency and enoughness of Christ.

Voices in culture try to tell us that we are enough and can solve our own problems. Culture says:

You are enough.
You are powerful.
You are strong.
Live your truth.

Voices in culture lie to us. They try to convince us to believe the pipe dream that perfection is out there just waiting to be discovered through a self-help blog, social media influencer, or by "finally just loving yourself."

But it's not working, is it? But it's not because we aren't trying. I mean, let's be honest. We've made the efforts.

- Hours of analyzing our personality types
- Idolizing self-care over biblical repentance
- Just "doing us" by doing whatever seems right in our eyes
- Trying to manifest our own truth

We've tried to achieve results on our own and we're miserable.

The topic of moralism by behavior modification has been around for decades and people are obsessed with obtaining it. So why aren't we all happier and more confident?

Allie Beth Stuckey says it like this, "Because the self can't be both the problem and the solution. If our problem is that we're insecure or unfulfilled, we're not going to be able to find the antidote to these things in the same place our insecurities and fears are coming from."[3]

The answer cannot be found within ourselves because what is broken simply cannot fix itself.

A few years ago, I had a Nissan Altima that I loved. She wasn't a looker, but she always got me from point A to point B and for that, I was grateful. One day, I looked down and realized that the "check engine" light was on. I didn't know how long it had been there (I'm not the best at noticing those kinds of things), but from what I could see on the surface, my car seemed to be working fine. So like any other responsible twenty-two-year-old, I kept living my life, hoping that somehow the light would go away and that my car would keep working properly.

And just like magic, one day the light did go off! *Whoa!* Did my car just fix itself? It was a miracle.

Until the next day when the light came right back on. I'm embarrassed to say, but this started a cycle for about six months where the light would go off for days, sometimes even weeks, and I would pretend as if the car was fine. But deep down, I knew better. I just didn't have the responsibility to face it and take care of what I knew was broken.

As you can probably guess, this story doesn't end well. One day, traveling to go see a friend who lived six hours away, I found myself stranded on the side of the road after my car stalled out. I ended up having to get it towed and the cost to fix it would ultimately be too much for me to save the car and I had to get rid of it for good.

I'll never forget when the mechanic said to me, "How long has the light been on? If you had brought it in when it first came on, you could have avoided this entire thing."

My wishful thinking that led to my avoidance was never going to pay off. Why? Because what is broken cannot fix itself.

When it comes to our struggles, we can't be both the problem and the solution. Contrary to the "enough" movement that is all over social media, we need a source outside ourselves to come in, invade our space, and heal the broken parts of our hearts and lives. Only then can we walk in newness, redemption, and purity.

> At the end of ourselves is **the beginning of Jesus' redemptive work** in the hearts of women in this generation just looking to be seen, known, and loved.

So what's the antidote if the self can't be both the problem and the solution? How do we stop drowning in failed attempts at perfectionism that ultimately have led so many of us to years and years of returning to the same brokenness?

The antidote is perfection. It's just not ours.

The antidote is Jesus.

What if the one thing you're trying to white-knuckle your way past (which is not feeling enough) is right where God wants you? What if it's right there that our flourishing begins?

At the end of ourselves is the beginning of Jesus' redemptive work in the hearts of women in this generation just looking to be seen, known, and loved.

Stuckey goes on to say, "There's a reason that Jesus describes himself as Living Water and Bread of Life: he satisfies. The searching for peace and for purpose stops in him alone. He created us; therefore only he can tell us who we are and why we're here."[4]

Not social media.

Not a relationship.

Not your best friend.

Not even yourself.

Him alone.

I get asked all the time how I knew Ryan was who I was meant to spend my life with. And no, it wasn't the tall, dark, and handsome part (of course, it didn't hurt!). What I tell people is that this relationship was just different. What made it different from my past relationships was that we were both living surrendered lives to Jesus when we met. No, we weren't perfect. No one is.

Our relationship had moments of confusion, messiness, and having to seek forgiveness from God and each other. But Ryan was fighting for all the right things: purity, accountability, truth, biblical manhood. And I was right there running at the same pace as I also fought to live as a new creation.

I knew I wanted to marry him not by all the ways he got it right, but by what he did when he got it wrong. The difference was this: when we failed, we sought Jesus, not justification. We didn't look to each other for our identities—we knew who we were and whose we were. When our eyes finally met, they'd been locked on Jesus and would stay there as we joined our lives together.

We must be women who set our gaze on Jesus, the author and

perfecter of our faith. Through Him, we can begin to see true life change and transformation.

And friend, God does see you. He sees your desires. He sent His Son to show you just how much He sees you. But until we know *how* He sees us, we will not be able to see ourselves as beloved daughters of the King. In the next chapter, we are going to look at four main ways that Jesus interacts specifically with women. Through that, we can begin to see our worth, our value, and a true glimpse into how the Father actually sees us.

PART 3

the tools to find
freedom

letting jesus
heal your wounds

remember one of the first children's Christian hymns I ever learned in Sunday school. Maybe you know it too. It goes like this:

Jesus loves me, this I know,
for the Bible tells me so.
Little ones to Him belong;
They are weak, but He is strong.
Yes, Jesus loves me!
Yes, Jesus loves me!
Yes, Jesus loves me!
The Bible tells me so.

I can still hear my Sunday school class sing this song all together. I sang with such confidence that it was true. I just loved it, and I loved the lyrics. I mean, who doesn't love being loved? I sure do. I'm guessing you do too. We all have this desire to be seen, known, and loved.

As we get older and experience more life, opening ourselves up to love can feel absolutely terrifying over time. As Tim Keller explains, "To be loved but not known is comforting but superficial. To be known and not loved is our greatest fear. But to be fully known and truly loved is, well, a lot like being loved by God. It is what we need more than anything."[1]

Although I didn't fully grasp how true these lyrics were at five years old in my Sunday school class, I understand now that the Bible *actually does tell us so.* The Word of God is full of Jesus' love for us. And, until we dig deep into Scripture and pull out some of the themes and intentionality of Jesus toward women, we will have a thin understanding and shallow belief that we are indeed known and loved by our Creator.

JESUS AND WOMEN IN SCRIPTURE

In my study on how Jesus moved toward women in Scripture, I came across four ways that we see the true essence of our Savior—God Incarnate. These four interactions lay the foundation for how we can view our relationship with Him.

They also set the stage for how we should expect to be treated when it comes to romantic relationships. Because when we discover the depth of love Jesus has for us, only then can we begin to open ourselves up to being known and loved by another human being. Jesus first, relationships second. Always.

> When we discover **the depth of Jesus' love for us,** only then can we open ourselves up to being known and loved by another human being.

Through these interactions, we don't just see Jesus. We can also see ourselves in these women on the receiving end of each encounter—especially if we have a past. Buckle up, friend! You're in really good company.

Interaction #1: Jesus, the One Who Pursues You
(John 4:1–30: The Woman at the Well)

In John 4, we meet our first friend. We don't know her name, but we learn a lot about her and Jesus from this conversation surrounding a water source:

> A woman from Samaria came to draw water. Jesus said to her, "Give me a drink." (For his disciples had gone away into the city to buy food.) The Samaritan woman said to him, "How is it that you, a Jew, ask for a drink from me, a woman of Samaria?" (For Jews have no dealings with Samaritans.) Jesus answered her, "If you knew the gift of God, and who it is that is saying to you, 'Give me a drink,' you would have asked him, and he would have given you living water." (John 4:7–10)

That's only the beginning of her interaction with Jesus. I encourage you to read the rest of her beautiful story in John 4:11–30. But here's what we learn about her from her time with Jesus.

She was culturally seen as "lesser than" because she was a Samaritan. Being one meant that she was generally hated by Jews for religious and racial reasons. One commentary goes as far as to say that Jews saw Samaritans as "half-breeds" due to being half Jew, half Gentile.[2] On top of that, Samaritans were known for having unstable theological beliefs, not fully rooted in Scripture. All of this is the perfect storm for prejudice and cultural tension between these two people groups.

Also, she struggled with shame and isolation. We see in verse 6 that she came at the "sixth hour," meaning around noon. Culturally, women would travel in groups in the early morning hours (the coolest time of the day) to draw water from the well. But our friend not only showed up at the hottest hour of the day, but she also came alone.

When we feel shame, we pull away from God and from others. Isolation is one of the biggest tools the enemy uses to keep us in our thought patterns of shame, guilt, and regret. That's where we find her. That's right where Jesus found her. And He had something to say about it.

Lastly, she had a questionable past when it came to relationships. "The woman answered him, 'I have no husband.' Jesus said to her, 'You are right in saying, "I have no husband" for you have had five husbands, and the one you now have is not your husband. What you have said is true'" (John 4:17–18).

> Isolation is one of **the biggest tools the enemy uses** to keep us in our thought patterns of shame, guilt, and regret.

When we're not rooted in Jesus, we have no idea what to look for. Our friend here had men give her attention, maybe even fulfill certain desires that she had (to be loved, to be taken care of, to be seen), but she was never truly satisfied because no man could ever give her what she truly longed for. She was looking for a love that stayed. A love that wasn't based on emotions and feelings but on commitment and Christ. She was looking for living water. And although she hadn't yet found it, the Living Water found her.

Here's what we learn about Jesus.

Jesus will take the unlikely path to pursue you. Because of the cultural hostility that the Jews had toward Samaritans, Jewish people typically didn't travel through Samaria when going from Judea to Galilee. Culturally, the hate was so real that they took the long route just to avoid the entire town. The tension was also real. But see here that Jesus didn't take the path most others took. Instead, verse 4 says, "And he had to pass through Samaria." This was a "had to" not out of a place of obligation or expectation but out of necessity to reach her.

Jesus will take any route He needs to take to get to your heart and your hurts. Not only did He take the unlikely route here, but He also waited for her. We see here that Jesus is willing, able, and eager to wait for us. Just like He was with this woman, He's abundantly patient and never late for an encounter with His children.

Next, Jesus will break any barrier to pursue you. It's important that we understand the role that women played in society in that day. They were seen as the lowest class. So on top of being not just a Samaritan, but a Samaritan woman, sister-friend didn't have a whole lot going for her. The Jewish religious leaders took this so seriously that in public, it was highly frowned upon for a rabbi to even speak to his wife or daughter. But we see here that Jesus wasn't too concerned with cultural barriers when it came to pursuing those He was after.

"Jesus said to her, 'Give me a drink'" (John 4:7). Not only did Jesus speak to her, but He humbled Himself to ask her for something. He knew they were going to have a hard conversation, and He wanted her to know that she had a Savior who wasn't afraid to get on her level and meet her where she was.

Lastly, Jesus will enter into your mess to pursue you. Are there parts of your life that just feel messy? Unhinged? Falling apart? Me too. Same for our friend here. She had parts of her life that she would probably do anything to hide. But Jesus wasn't afraid of those areas. On the contrary, those were the exact areas He was excited to dig into with her.

I'm not proud of this, but I'm a pretty messy person by nature. I remember when Ryan and I were engaged, so many people would warn me that living with a boy is messy and that I better prepare myself. I rarely commented back, but I always remember thinking, *Actually, I feel bad for Ryan that he has to live with me.* Yes, I am the messy one in our marriage.

One of the main messes that I make is what I like to call "my piles." If you are a pile maker, you know what these are. They are piles of clothes.

After trying on multiple outfits a day, I will form a pile in a corner of our room instead of hanging those clothes up. It's become a running joke because if Ryan sees a pile, he can't understand how it could be anything but dirty clothes. But with lots of patience, I explain to him that there is a difference between a clean pile and a dirty pile. In fact, most of my piles are clean! It's a real problem, and I'm working on it, okay?

I think sometimes we also compartmentalize the messy part of our lives. We have the "not so bad piles," the "dirty piles," and even the "looks clean on the outside piles." But at the end of the day, a pile is a pile. And Jesus came to enter into our piles, no matter how dirty or put-together they may seem. If something isn't where He calls it to be, He will enter in and address it—even the piles we're afraid for anyone to see.

> We each have hard areas where Jesus is sitting, waiting, and ready to be welcomed.

That's what He did here with our friend at the well. He wasn't afraid to have the hard conversations about her relationships. He addressed the reality of her past without judgment or heaping shame onto her. Just like her pile of past broken relationships, we each have hard areas that Jesus is sitting, waiting, and ready to be welcomed in.

Know this: Jesus will never enter a situation that He doesn't fully plan to redeem. His pursuit always has purpose. Let Him into the hard piles, the messy piles, and even the piles you've come to accept, and watch what He'll do.

Relationship Tip: Single sis, look for a man who pursues you with this heart posture as well. No, he won't be perfect like Jesus. He will blow it at times. He might struggle to hear the truth about your past, but a true Jesus-following man will pursue you with the gentleness, intentionality, and humility we see modeled here through Christ. A great pursuit is worth waiting for. And for my married friends, if you aren't being pursued like you desire, the best gift you could give your spouse is to pray for them. Pray specifically. Pray boldly. Pray with belief that God can instill in them a heart of pursuit toward you and the things of God.

Interaction #2: Jesus, the One Who Stops
(Luke 8:42b-48: The Woman in the Crowd)

I'm not sure which truth it will be for you, but for whatever reason, this part of Jesus is the hardest truth for me to believe. When my dad died, this was the biggest lie that the enemy used when it came to taking the time to process, grieve, and heal. It was like he was whispering in my ear, "Time doesn't stop for you. You better keep on going." Maybe something has happened in your life where you felt like you had to keep going, even with a broken spirit. For me, this caused years of undealt-with brokenness and hurt that I got really good at hiding. But I can now look back and see that this was a lie. Jesus shows us otherwise.

As we've learned in previous chapters, the quickest way to point out lies is to *know truth*. Truth is and will always be our greatest weapon. Truth about the essence of Jesus is found here in our next interaction between Him and a woman who had walked in shame and hiding for years. If you feel just like someone in the crowd, unseen and invisible, the story of this woman is for you.

As Jesus went, the people pressed around him. And there was a woman who had had a discharge of blood for twelve years, and though she had spent all her living on physicians, she could not be healed by anyone. She came up behind him and touched the fringe of his garment, and immediately her discharge of blood ceased. And Jesus said, "Who was it that touched me?" When all denied it, Peter said, "Master, the crowds surround you and are pressing in on you!" But Jesus said, "Someone touched me, for I perceive that power has gone out from me." And when the woman saw that she was not hidden, she came trembling, and falling down before him declared in the presence of all the people why she had touched him, and how she had been immediately healed. And he said to her, "Daughter, your faith has made you well; go in peace." (Luke 8:42b–48)

For some of us, we can't imagine suffering for twelve whole years. For some of you, that's half of your entire life. For others, twelve years seems short compared to how long you've felt hidden, broken, or deeply wounded by something. For our friend here, she had to face something daily that reminded her to stay hidden.

We don't know what caused this bleeding, but I can guess that because of this disease, she was completely closed off to anyone seeing her as she was—especially men. Culturally, Jewish law stated that a woman who had any sort of bleeding was deemed "unclean" and unable to touch anyone or have anyone touch her for seven days, in order to avoid imparting her uncleanliness to them (Lev. 15:19–30). Additionally, when it came to women's roles in society, if she wasn't married, she was seen as useless and less than. (It looks different today, but a lot of our internal battles struggle with this same lie.)

In our hurried and overwhelmed modern culture, our society as a whole has lost the art of stopping for people who are in need. Because to stop for others in need, we have to be present enough to see when someone we love (or even someone we don't know) might be struggling. On the flip side, I think if I were to ask you when the last time you felt like someone really paused their daily routine to listen or help you in your time of need, some of you would have to really think hard. Because of this, it's really difficult to remember how much Jesus longs to stop for you. But He does. And He doesn't just stop to listen. He also stops to redeem you in three significant ways.

Jesus stops to show you that He's never too busy for you. We all have our pet peeves that we get uptight about. For Ryan, his is smacking food. He can't stand it. For me, it's being late. It's not that I care much about if people are late when meeting up with me. I just can't handle it when I'm the one late. This, for me, leads often to a rushed and non-present spirit. When I speed through my day out of a place of just wanting to avoid being late, I can easily miss what God has for me in the moment I'm in. Do you relate? We so often rush through our day, going from one task to another without batting an eye. The problem is that instead of remembering why we're on earth, we start to make tasks out of people. But people aren't tasks. People are people—God's beloved and His highest priority.

So why do we sacrifice people's needs every day on the altar of our to-do lists and agendas? Why are we obsessed with maintaining an image of importance to those around us?

Ultimately, it comes down to pride, the opposite of humility. The opposite of Jesus.

Phillippians 2:3–8 gives us a different model to follow:

> Do nothing from selfish ambition or conceit, but in humility count others more significant than yourselves. Let each of you look not only to his own interests, but also to the interests of others. Have this mind among yourselves, which is yours in Christ Jesus, who, though he was in the form of God, did not count equality with God a thing to be grasped, but emptied himself, by taking the form

of a servant, being born in the likeness of men. And being found in human form, he humbled himself by becoming obedient to the point of death, even death on a cross.

As Jesus was on the way to change another young girl's life (more on that in a bit), He—in humility—didn't care how others saw Him. In fact, He was being rushed at that moment by people who were seen as "important," but He knew that the value of human life comes only from the Father, not man. So what did He do? He refused to keep going out of a place of busyness to show her that He always has time for us when we're hurting. God is not hurried. Even in our hectic and chaotic world, we have a God who isn't too busy to hear our hearts and hold our tears.

> Even in our hectic and chaotic world, **we have a God who isn't too busy** to hear our hearts and hold our tears.

Jesus stops for you to remind you of your identity. When most people read this story, they often focus on the miracle of physical healing, which is absolutely beautiful. But there is an even more beautiful moment that is a greater miracle than just physical freedom. It's identity freedom.

See, when she was still hidden and touched the fringe of Jesus' robe, she was healed. But that was only half the healing. After Jesus refused to continue without looking the person in the face who had touched Him, she finally came forward. She stepped into the light. She had a turning point of boldness, even in her fear, to step forward. Even in that fear, she took the leap to be seen. And how did Jesus respond? With the sweetest words that we could ever hear from our Creator. The one word that makes a million other false identities melt away.

"And he said to her, 'Daughter, your faith has made you well; go in peace'" (Luke 8:48, emphasis added).

That day, she not only received relief from twelve years of pain, but she also received healing from what I believe was a lifetime of misplaced identity.

When God stops for us, it is always for the purpose of reminding us or reestablishing who and whose we are. Until we slow down and embrace the God who has slowed down for us, we won't be able to hear through the crowd of voices when Jesus whispers "daughter" over us.

My encouragement to you: slow down, get quiet, and be reminded of your truest and primary identity—daughter.

Jesus stops to actually heal you. Jesus didn't just stop that day in the crowd to be a great listening ear. He stopped to take action. He stopped to heal. Speaking of healing, what a perfect segway into interaction #3 . . .

Relationship Tip: Single sis, wait for a guy who stops for you and takes the time to understand your story without casting judgment. Like this woman, your truest identity will always be "daughter." Don't settle for a guy who isn't willing to sit in the hard moments with you and remind you of who you are in Christ. And my married girls, it's never too late to start having those conversations with your spouse that give you both space to hold one another's stories. Are there parts of your past that have gone unshared? Pray for the time and space to open up within your marriage.

Interaction #3: Jesus, the One Who Heals You
(Luke 8:41-42a; 49-55a: Jairus' Daughter)

Our next interaction with a young woman comes on the bookends of the encounter with the woman in the crowd. The reason Jesus was in the crowd that day was because He was heading somewhere—to see about another daughter and continue being the great healer that He is.

And there came a man named Jairus, who was a ruler of the synagogue. And falling at Jesus' feet, he implored him to come to his house, for he had an only daughter, about twelve years of age, and she was dying. . . . While he was still speaking, someone from the ruler's house came and said, "Your daughter is dead; do not trouble the Teacher any more." But Jesus on hearing this answered him, "Do not fear; only believe, and she will be well." And when he came to the house, he allowed no one to enter with him, except Peter and John and James, and the father and mother of the child. And all were weeping and mourning for her, but he said, "Do not weep, for she is not dead but sleeping." And they laughed at him, knowing that she was dead. But taking her by the hand he called, saying, "Child, arise." And her spirit returned, and she got up at once. (Luke 8:41–42, 49–55)

So often, we read about healing in the Bible, but in the twenty-first century, we don't have a lot of radical belief that God can and will actually heal. A big reason for this is that there has been a lot of hurt through the years on the topic of healing. I've talked to a lot of people who have prayed *big* prayers for a family member or friend to be healed of a sickness, and the story didn't end in healing on earth. It ended in death.

I once heard a story of a man who grew up in a small church where his dad was the pastor. When he was only eight years old, his dad got sick with cancer and the elder of the church rallied the congregation together to pray that God would heal him and take away the cancer. Day and night people were at their house praying. Scared and feeling alone, he retreated to his bedroom and didn't attend some of the prayer nights. Months later, his dad's cancer grew and he passed away. Feeling devastated, it made matters worse when one of the elders said to him in a private conversation, "It was because of you that your father died. If you had only had more faith, your father would have been healed." For good reason, this statement caused years and years of confusion toward the topic of healing.

But as we just saw with Jesus' interactions with the woman in the crowd and Jairus' daughter, God's Son was sent to be the great physician. So much so that there are twenty-two stories of healing recorded in the synoptic gospels (Matthew, Mark, and Luke).[3]

When we trust God to heal, He will heal. But here's the deal: if we trust the God whose ways and thoughts are higher than ours (Isa. 55:9), we have to trust that sometimes He will heal in ways that we can't always understand.

Healing in hopeless situations is what Jesus is best at.

For my dad, who passed away when I was just starting out my teen years, I truly believe that healing came in the form of God calling him to heaven. Even on the days I can't understand why he couldn't stay here with me, I fight to trust that God is both a healer *and* sovereign over the form of healing.

We see in this passage that when all seemed hopeless, Jesus brought healing. *Healing in hopeless situations is what Jesus is best at.*

To everyone in the room that day, the little girl was dead. What was seen was the end of the road. What was seen brought tears and mourning. What was seen was hopelessness.

What men saw was death. What Jesus saw was an opportunity to have His power rest on a young woman for whom God had mapped out a "future and a hope" (Jer. 29:11). What Jesus saw was healing.

Healing isn't just for biblical times. The healing power of Jesus still exists and is available to us today. Healing can come in the form of:

- Physical healing
- Emotional healing

- Shame healing
- Trauma healing
- Relational healing
- Spiritual healing

What area is it for you? I encourage you to circle the one above that you are most desperate for in your life right now. Jesus is the author of healing, and He extends an invitation for us to pray boldly for Him to bring healing. It moves the heart of Jesus to hear you believe Him for miraculous healing. Whether it's for you or someone you love, Jesus loves to hear your cries of belief for Him to do what the eye cannot imagine or see in the moment.

These are scary prayers, after all. It's hard to pray in full belief for healing, and then it does not happen. But we must trust in a God who sees the whole picture when we only see a sliver of what He might be doing under the surface.

With tears in our eyes, just like Jairus, let's contend and believe for healing and, with open hands, cry out. "For now we see in a mirror dimly, but then face to face. Now I know in part; then I shall know fully, even as I have been fully known" (1 Cor. 13:12). Regardless of the outcome, let us cry out that it is well with our souls.

Relationship Tip: Single sis, start learning now that a guy is not your savior or your healer. Only Jesus is. Look to Jesus to heal what only He can heal and look for a guy who stands beside you. Look for someone with the spirit of Jairus, contending to Jesus on behalf of you for healing. Married sis, even the best of husbands can't be your savior. Letting Jesus be your satisfaction over your husband can lead to greater enjoyment and appreciation of one another.

Interaction #4: Jesus, the One Who Sees You
(John 7:53–8:11: The Woman Caught in Adultery)

This is by far my favorite story of the four. That's kind of a strange thing to say considering the nature of the story, and if I'm honest, it kind of makes me sweat a little, but it's just so profound, and we learn *so* much about Jesus' grace and kindness toward us as beloved daughters.

The first thing we need to acknowledge here is that we can safely assume that a man also was involved in this sexual act—yet he was not brought before Jesus to be judged. Just the woman. I can't imagine how ashamed she must have felt, lying there, naked, exposed, and facing condemnation.

In relationships, we often feel the same twinge today when it comes to sex and boundaries. And friend, we do have a part to play. God has given us bodies that men find attractive and, because of that, we can use that to cause men to stumble. We should be aware of that and seek discernment on what honoring God looks like with our bodies. But at the same time, because of the fall in Genesis 3, men also struggle with passivity. It is what has led to so many guys out there, even well-meaning guys trying to follow Jesus, unwilling to set boundaries in relationships. We need to see that Jesus has a better plan and design for us when it comes to this sex complex.

On top of the shame she felt, there was also a very real sense of fear. As we read, the Law of Moses states that a woman caught in adultery was to be stoned. This capital offense under Jewish law held no mercy for this woman.

This was what many of the religious leaders were waiting for. Because, in reality, they didn't really care about the woman or even the consequences. Their main target was actually Jesus. This woman, even in her sin, was simply collateral damage in the Pharisees' dysfunction. Theologian William Barclay explains it like this: "They were not looking on this woman as a person at all; they were looking on her only as a thing, an instrument whereby they could formulate a charge against Jesus."[4]

But what the world might see as damaged goods to be tossed aside, Jesus saw as His prized possession.

The Pharisees were after Jesus. But Jesus was seeking after her.

After they had put Jesus in a position to entrap Him, He did something absolutely brilliant. *He stooped down.*

Theologians speculate many different reasons as to why Jesus stooped down and what He was actually writing in the dirt that day. But the most important question we can ask in this scene is, "Who was Jesus there for?" He wasn't there for the Pharisees. He wasn't there for Himself. He was there for the woman.

> When we can't stand to face what we've done, **Jesus humbles Himself** and gets in the dirt and mess with us.

The woman who was slumped in the dirt, exposed, awaiting stoning—a potential death sentence.

I imagine as she lay there with Pharisees yelling at her, she had no strength in her shame to lift her head. When we are overcome with something we've done, it often feels like the only thing we can do is to slump our heads and embrace the weight of our actions. It seems nearly impossible to look up. But Jesus didn't ask her to. Instead, He came down.

We see here that when we can't find the strength to reach out to Jesus, He will always reach for us. When we can't stand to face what we've done, Jesus humbles Himself and gets in the dirt and mess with us. That's where healing began for her. And that's where it begins for us.

No one fully knows why Jesus stooped down. But if you can exercise what I like to call your "holy imagination" with me for a moment, what if one of the possible reasons Jesus lowered Himself was because it was the only place He could get to her? To meet her gaze? To show her that even in her shame, He truly saw, knew, and loved her.

And as each man, from the oldest to youngest, slowly faded away, Jesus stayed there, with a presence that assured her that she was safe and that He wasn't going anywhere.

This is the gospel, friend. We have a God who knows we don't have what it takes to make it to Him. We are too fallen, and that's okay. When Jesus got on her level that day, He displayed what His whole purpose on earth was: *to put on flesh to be with us* (John 1:14). He longs to do for you what He did for her. To get on your level, look you in the eye, and whisper, "Neither do I condemn you; go, and from now on sin no more" (John 8:11).

Jesus wants to encounter us so that He can free us with His extravagant, unmerited, perfect grace. And, in this story and our stories, this life of grace all starts with a gaze.

A. W. Tozer said it best. He wrote, "When we lift our inward eyes to gaze upon God we are sure to meet friendly eyes gazing back at us, for it is written that the eyes of the Lord run to and fro throughout all the earth. The sweet language of experience is 'Thou God seest me.' When the eyes of the soul looking out meet the eyes of God looking in, heaven has begun right here on this earth."[5]

What I love most about this woman's story is that Jesus did not speak a word to her until every last person had left. I think Jesus knew that in order to truly hear Him and meet His gaze, she must have the other voices of the world quieted first.

The same is true for us. Only once you and I quiet the noise, will we hear His whispers loud and clear over us. It's in that secret, sacred space that we might be able to finally hear, "You are pursued. You are My daughter. You are healed. You are always seen."

Relationship Tip: Single friends, pray for a guy who sees you as Jesus does. Find someone who understands that we are all sinners in need of grace and that forgiveness is offered to us all, equally. And to my married friends, what if it's time to take the first step in seeing yourself this way? When we take Jesus at His word that our identity is made new, we will start to live a life of freedom and redemption that can impact our marriages.

STEPPING INTO THE LIGHT

It wasn't until I experienced this Jesus that my life started to shift in the secret places, and I began to welcome the invitation to see myself as "daughter." Because of this sweet season with Jesus, I also started to realize that, just like the woman at the well and the one caught in adultery, there were parts of my life that I feared being exposed. Just like Jairus' daughter, I needed new life. And just like the woman in the crowd, I needed to reach out and receive healing—both from Jesus and in the presence of others.

Like some of these women, there were secrets hidden under the surface that I had never brought to the light with others. There were memories in my past that I had never told anyone. So I started to ask God what to do with all of it. I promised Him that I would take any step necessary to bring what's hidden into the light. For myself. For my growing relationship with Ryan. Most importantly, for Jesus.

And that's what led me to the day that everything changed.

CHAPTER 8

why you need community

As a perk of living near Nashville, I'm surrounded by so many incredible singers. And full disclosure, I don't happen to be one of them. I don't say that in a self-deprecating way, but singing just isn't one of ya girl's gifts. I think I can carry the slightest bit of a tune, but as far as a God-given gift to be used and displayed for His glory? Well, I'll let my friends take that one.

I have a few friends specifically that every time I am with them, I ask if they will sing with me. Yes, I am that friend. Because yes, my friends can sing, but even more than that, they have the gift of harmonizing with just about anyone. So what I make them do is listen to my record-scratching voice, blend their voice with mine, and somehow make me (just for a moment) sound half decent. For people who can't really sing, you know what I'm talking about! It's fun to sing with someone so good that they drown you out enough to make you feel halfway decent for just a chorus or two. Everyone needs a musically talented friend to discover the thrill of harmony.

I think harmonizing is one of the most spectacular things on earth. To pick up on someone else's tone and offset it in such a way that two voices blend to form a new sound is nothing short of heavenly to me. But just like a lot of things in life, harmony can't happen alone.

Harmony is known as "a consistent, orderly, or pleasing arrangement of parts; congruity,"[1] and needs at least two to pull off. It isn't possible with just one individual. Don't get me wrong, I've seen solo performances in my life that have brought me to tears, but they still don't touch two or more people singing together to create a new sound that couldn't otherwise have been created alone.

> Community—or simply put, friendship—in its correct form is the perfect picture of harmony.

I believe that all creation points back to God's good design, and harmony is no exception. The apostle Paul uses the metaphor of harmony when it comes to God's design for community: "Rejoice with those who rejoice, weep with those who weep. Live in harmony with one another" (Rom. 12:15–16a). Community—or simply put, friendship—in its correct form is the perfect picture of harmony.

THE ORIGINAL COMMUNITY

When it came to community, I operated as a solo artist for many, many years. Even years I was walking with Jesus, I didn't truly link up with others who might come alongside me to create something beautiful. On the outside, you might have always seen me with friends, but on the inside were walls, unhealthy boundaries, and a guarded heart. I refused to step into something that God requires of us in order to live out the beautiful design He has created for us.

I think at the root of this was fear. I was afraid of being known. Fearful of being judged by some of the details of my life. Afraid of being rejected once people knew about the "real me." Because at my core, I so desired friends to walk with me and know me, but I also feared being rejected by that same good gift.

Do you know when the first community was formed? It wasn't Mesopotamia, Egypt, or even God's chosen Jewish people. The first community was actually one that wasn't formed at all. It just was.

Isaiah laid out the eternality of the Trinity years before Jesus set foot on earth: "'Draw near to me, hear this: from the beginning I have not spoken in secret, from the time it came to be I have been there.' And now the Lord God has sent me, and his Spirit" (Isa. 48:16).

The Trinity consisting of the perfect community of God the Father, God the Son, and God the Holy Spirit is the original community. A community that depends on each other, accomplishes more together than separately, and is perfect and lacking in nothing in and of itself. The perfect harmony.

Friend, if the Creator of the universe sees it fully fit to exist in community and live in harmony, how much more do you and I need our people to walk through life with?

THE FEAR OF LETTING SOMEONE IN

As my relationship with Ryan grew stronger and became more serious, he and I started to have very real conversations about our lives before meeting each other. The daunting reality of sharing with him (or anyone) at that point some of the details of my past weighed on me in a way that you can only understand if you struggle with shame. With the growth of our relationship, the increasing dread of exposing the reality of my past also became all the more real. I knew that Ryan's history wasn't like mine. As believers, we know and believe that all sin is equal, but the details of my story just felt heavier.

I had brought my past to Jesus, and through that, I experienced very real healing and redemption before I even met Ryan. And I was so grateful for that. But in this new season, knowing that this man would likely become my husband, I felt God calling me into the next phase of my healing journey. A phase that included me letting not just Ryan in but also other trusted friends in.

I knew that my healing wasn't going to come from sharing all the details with Ryan while still living in secret to the trusted women of God that He had brought into my life. I also knew if I didn't let someone in, I was selling Ryan and myself short of a life of freedom God was offering me.

That Sunday at church, my pastor spoke on this exact topic. Coincidence? I think not. God always has a way of placing us right where we need to be in order to hear and receive what we need for that day. He said, "Everybody needs somebody who knows everything." It truly hit me that I didn't have one person in my life who knew everything about my past. And I think there were reasons why I didn't let others into my life, and why you may not either

One of those reasons, of course, is shame. If the enemy can keep us hidden in our pasts, he will continue to write this narrative over our life: "If someone knew the whole truth, they wouldn't love you." Given our greatest God-given desire to be known and loved, this is more than enough to keep our pasts wrapped in perfectly packaged fig leaves.

Another reason we don't let people in is because we don't believe we are worth the time. Even to the friends who have gone out of their way to show us that we matter, we are so slow to believe it. We see those we love for their worth, true identity, and value, but it is the hardest thing in the world to see it in ourselves.

I was once on a plane with a friend who is truly one of the most loved people I have ever known. She lights up a room more than most people I know and has the gift of reminding people of their worth in Christ.

Halfway through the plane ride, she asked me if I had any gum. I pulled out my freshly opened pack and pulled out a piece to hand to her. She quickly said, "Can I just have a half piece of gum?" Without hesitating, I split it and handed her half to her.

As she started chewing it, it dawned on me how strange it was that she only wanted half a piece instead of the whole. I turned to her and asked her why she only wanted half. She explained to me that it wasn't a matter of not wanting the whole piece, but that in high school, there was a girl who always had a pack of gum on her. (You know, that type of girl from high school who always had the gum—a total power move if you ask me.) When my sweet friend would ask for a piece of gum, she would either refuse her request or, at best, offer her half a piece.

This small story totally broke my heart! My friend—the friend of all friends—was made to feel less than by a power play over a pack of gum. I looked at her and said, "You *are* worthy of a whole piece of gum!"

Don't we do this all the time in our friendships? We convince ourselves that we aren't valuable enough for someone to dedicate time and a listening ear to us to share our stories in order to live in freedom.

This was my story for as long as I can remember. I couldn't tell you why, but I've always feared being an inconvenience to anyone—ever. Some of my earliest memories include a few days when my mom would forget to give me lunch money before school in the third grade. I would go up to the front office, call her, and beg her to bring me money so I didn't have to borrow someone else's money that day. Although my mom would assure me that she would pay back the mom of the friend I would borrow from, I couldn't stand the thought of being a burden on someone in any form.

The enemy will do anything to convince us to stay hidden, believing that if someone saw the real us, we wouldn't be loved or accepted as we really are. Brennan Manning recalls this inner struggle to stay hidden with what he calls the "imposter":

The impostor within whispered, *Brennan, don't ever be your real self anymore, because nobody likes you as you are. Invent a new self that everybody will admire and nobody will know.* So I became a good boy—polite, well mannered, unobtrusive, and deferential. I studied hard, scored excellent grades, won a scholarship in high school, and was stalked every waking moment by the terror of abandonment and the sense that nobody was there for me.[2]

Although we as women are prone to doubt our value, God summons us to take the steps necessary for Him to (thankfully and gracefully) prove us wrong.

Despite every good reason I could come up with as to why I shouldn't call a friend, that day at church really challenged me to start with one person and let them know everything. And I mean everything. Every night. Every memory. Every ex that I had prayed to forget. It needed to come out. I needed to take the risk to be known and loved by God's people if I was really going to take the next step in my relationship with Ryan but, more importantly, my relationship with Jesus.

QUALITIES TO LOOK FOR IN COMMUNITY

As I prayed through who that person should be, there were a few characteristics of someone that quickly rose to the top of my list. These qualities are going to be important for us to look for as we take steps in being seen, known, and loved for where we've been and who we are.

1. Compassion

The first is compassion. Someone who is compassionate doesn't just listen to listen, but they listen to learn. They listen to care. They listen to meet us where we're at. We see such a clear biblical mandate from the apostle Peter when it comes to being people of compassion:

"Finally, all of you, be like-minded, be sympathetic, love one another, be compassionate and humble " (1 Peter 3:8 NIV).

Jesus displayed a heart of compassion throughout His time on earth, but the main recipients of His compassion were always people who were hurting or suffering. Matthew 9:36 shares, "When he [Jesus] saw the crowds, he had compassion on them, because they were harassed and helpless, like sheep without a shepherd" (NIV).

People of compassion care more about your healing than needing to be the one who brings about your healing. Compassion is selfless. Compassion is the basis for Christian community and the safe space where we find healing.

When you find a friend who has a genuine spirit of compassion, you've found a safe place.

2. Empathy

The next quality that I looked for when it came to sharing my past was empathy. *Empathy* is defined as "the ability to understand another person's feelings."[3] Empathy takes the leap from just "I see you" to "I'm with you."

I think so many people think that we can only have empathy if we've walked through similar situations, but in God's economy, we as believers have access to a Spirit who allows us to empathize with others by leaning in and being willing vessels to "bear one another's burdens, and so fulfill the law of Christ" (Gal. 6:2). Empathy comes with taking the space and time to hear the reason behind the tears in someone's eyes and softens our own hearts to see others the way Christ sees them.

I heard a story years ago about a highly respected professor who, in his later years, agreed to sit on a panel to share some of his greatest life lessons. When asked, "Is there anything you would have done differently?" He thought intently and fired off the most profound answer,

"No, but I would have done everything I did with more tears in my eyes."
What a beautiful thing it is to share in one another's burdens.

Not only that, but when we're met with empathy from a friend, we're able to display one of the most underestimated healing practices that God's given us: the space and freedom to cry. I'm not just speaking allegorically here. I'm talking about practicing actual crying in front of someone.

We're about to get into a little bit of a science lesson, so bear with me.

Did you know that when you cry, you release the stress hormone cortisol? In our lives, we carry so many stressors: in relationships, past hurts, harmful self-talk, false identities, finances, worries about our future, body image, and the list goes on. But God, in His amazing design, has given us a way to release our stress. Yes, spiritually, but also physically.

So when you cry emotional tears (not to be confused with tears caused by physical pain), your body releases cortisol. Incredible, right? But it gets even better. When you cry in front of a trusted person or friend, you release double the amount of cortisol.[4] Stress, pain, and shame actually start to heal when we take the brave step to be seen and known by a friend in our vulnerable state.

Wow. I love God's intentionality. He is showing us here that we need each other. We can't heal alone.

The author of Ecclesiastes reflects on this truth: "Two are better than one, because they have a good reward for their toil. For if they fall, one will lift up his fellow. But woe to him who is alone when he falls and has not another to lift him up! Again, if two lie together, they keep warm, but how can one keep warm alone?" (Eccl. 4:9–11).

Empathy is the bridge to which all healing can begin. Empathy grants permission to not just the good, but the bad and ugly.

3. Grace

The last one is grace. Grace is the essence of Christlikeness.

I once heard of an older couple who was the epitome of "couple goals" to everyone around them. Their community admired how they loved each other with compassion, empathy, and grace toward one another.

One particular story that made this couple so special was actually during a time when the husband hid some important information from his wife that eventually came to light and had the potential to cause a pretty massive divide between the two.

The wife had a choice to make: hold the grudge (as he rightfully deserved) or move toward him in forgiveness and grace. Although all she wanted to do was pack her things and leave, she took a different route.

She went to the grocery store.

Heading straight to the baking aisle, she picked out a bag of flour, sugar, baking soda, eggs, salt, and sprinkles (his favorite). And while he was at work, she baked him a cake.

When he arrived home, instead of being met with rage, he was met with the sweet aroma of a confetti cake and the even sweeter aroma of grace.

Stunned and slightly confused, his immediate reaction was to reject the cake and declare, "I don't deserve this or your forgiveness." She said, "I know, but this cake doesn't have to be earned. This is a grace cake." That night, they created space to share their hearts, cry together, and be reconciled as two sinners saved by grace.

This grace cake is a small picture of what has been done for us on the cross two thousand-plus years ago. We find the greatest display of love and our basis for a life saturated with grace in Ephesians: "For by grace you have been saved through faith. And this is not your own doing; it is the gift of God, not a result of works, so that no one may boast. For we are his workmanship, created in Christ Jesus for good works, which God prepared beforehand, that we should walk in them" (Eph. 2:8–10).

Jesus is the One who declares grace over us in our worst moments. And we, as the body of Christ, need friends who will listen to us, hand us a grace cake, and point us to One who paved the way with the finest ingredients to give us grace for yesterday, today, and forever.

THE FRIEND WE ALL NEED

Dane Ortlund sums up so beautifully the type of friend(s) we should look for when it comes to taking steps toward being recipients of compassion, empathy, and grace. He writes, "What does a friend do? A friend draws near in time of need. A friend delights to come into solidarity with us, bearing our burdens. A friend listens. A friend is available to us, never too high or important to give us time."[5]

And thanks be to God, I have that friend. Her name is Dottie. Dottie is the essence of the friend I have laid out in this chapter. She is quick to listen, slow to speak, and full of so much grace. Dottie's past is wildly different from mine, yet I knew she was filled with the spirit in a way that she would see me through the lens of grace, not condemnation.

On a random summer day in 2017, I called her up and asked if she would meet me at a coffee shop in Birmingham the weekend of a mutual friend's wedding we were attending. Even during a busy weekend, she didn't hesitate to say yes and carve out time. Right there, I was already grateful for the expression of Jesus she showed me.

We met up, ordered coffee and a homemade pop-tart to share, caught up momentarily, and then she silently waited for me to get started. She wasn't hurried, but she also wasn't going to let me small talk for two hours.

So I sat there, taking the leap of letting someone into my past. In some ways, even letting myself into the reality of some of the shame I had hidden for years.

Things came up in those two hours that I had forgotten were there. Things were said that I've never dared to utter out loud. Tears flooded in ways I didn't think were possible due to years of walls and fig leaves.

Truth is, I couldn't tell you one thing Dottie said to me in those two hours. But I will never forget the way she listened. The way she loved. The empathy in her eyes. The compassion in her nods. The grace in her posture.

That day, fig leaves fell and shriveled on the ground, which was fine because I didn't need them anymore.

How powerful is it that freedom can come with simply letting one person in? Yes, it was great to let Dottie in, but more than that, she ushered in an invitation for me to let Jesus in. She provided a small glimpse of El Roi—the God who sees me. That day in that random coffee shop, heaven and earth collided in my soul. When I walked out of those doors, I also walked out with a new sense of true freedom and became a more whole version of the daughter I was created to be.

We all need a Dottie. I encourage you to find your Dottie. When we find more people like Dottie, we will inevitably find more of Jesus.

Not only do we need community and safe people in our lives, but they need us too. Do you believe, in your life right now, that you could be used by God in some of these ways?

Even as I type about my friend, I can't help but long for someone, someday, to say these things about me. That I am a safe person. That I am a good listener. That I point people back to Jesus. And not for the sake of being that for someone, but for the sake of the very real broken hearts and hurting people out there who need real stories of hope. Yes, you need community, but community also needs you and your story of redemption.

WHY COMMUNITY NEEDS YOU

Through the years, I have heard a lot of great advice, encouragement, and truth. I have had the privilege of being in rooms with people who are wiser, more eloquent, and more Spirit-filled than I may ever be. But I think the most powerful and God-breathed phrase I have ever heard goes something like this: "Wow, you've struggled with that too? I thought I was the only one."

I used to be ashamed of my story. As you know, I wasn't just ashamed. I was hidden. It was this way for years. I couldn't fathom sharing my story with someone. But as I took those steps with people like Dottie, I realized that Jesus didn't want to just heal me. He wanted to usher in healing for others through my story.

I used to think it was a coincidence how many people I came in contact with who had lost a father, struggled with habitual sexual impurity, or who felt too far gone to live the life God had for them. Then it dawned on me that God knows exactly what He's doing. He knows who to bring into our lives and when. Yes, for us, but also for them.

Our stories, our past, when handed over to Him to redeem, serve as an act of worship to the goodness and the power of the living God in our lives. There isn't a measure of freedom that God will offer to one of His children that He won't make accessible to all. God does not withhold freedom, joy, redemption, or the reckless abandonment kind of love.

The kingdom needs your story, friend.

I'll never forget a few years ago when I was asked to share some of my story with a small group of girls who were studying women in the Word together. I felt called to not just skirt around my past with phrases like "struggled with sexual impurity," but I knew God was calling me to share the exact details of where I had been so that God can display the actual details of where He's brought me.

So I shared. In detail. I shared numbers, certain nights, and ended with how exactly God had redeemed me. Step by step. It was messy. It was pretty awkward. But I knew it was a safe space where the altar could be laid out for redemption to be received by specific women in that living room. I didn't know who, but I knew they were there.

When sharing your story, it's important to know your audience. Some parts of your story aren't beneficial to share at certain times. This doesn't mean you're still living in shame of what's happened, but there is a level of discernment in knowing what is beneficial to share and when. For example, I probably won't share from a stage or with a room of women that I don't know the things I shared that night in detail. This isn't because I want to keep it hidden, but there's a time and space. For me, that was a time and space I felt called, and I put it out there, hoping that my story could be a pathway to someone else's freedom.

And boy, was it. One of the girls came up to me afterward, and I could tell she wanted to talk with me. We found a corner of the house, and she shared with me that her past was very similar to mine, and she hadn't heard anyone open up like that, especially when it came to sexual sin. She also said she had never heard a story of redemption like mine. It wasn't because there aren't a ton of redemption stories out there, but God knew she needed to hear mine.

She told me it had been a tough year for her. She knew Jesus, but she had been giving herself away and hanging out with friends who did the same. She expressed she wanted to make a change and that God really used my story to give her the courage and desire to turn from those ways of living. I'm not saying it was just because of that night, but I watched my college friend start to run in a different direction that night. I saw her grow in an abiding love for Jesus that ended up changing the trajectory of her life in the most redemptive ways.

Don't just let God into your story. Let Him into the sharing of your story for the edification and healing story of others too. *Every area means every area.*

Even if one person is impacted by your story in your community, it's worth it. As children of God, He gives us the permission to care enough about the "one" as Jesus did to live boldly and declare the Lord's goodness in our testimonies.

People need your story. We all love to be poured into, but there comes the point in our Christian maturation journey where we must shift from just being the one invested in to the one investing in the younger generations. Don't get me wrong. We will always need both. We will never arrive at a point where we don't desperately need to be heard and loved, but if you are in Christ, there is a personal responsibility to add value to your Christian community by being passionate about seeing life change in those around you.

> Through Jesus' life, **we have everything we need and more** to show up, do the hard work of healing, and let God start to use us for His glory.

The enemy wants to conceal your healing. Jesus wants to heal your concealing. Remember, the greatest tool Satan has is isolation. But Jesus wants to open the floodgates of a generation that declares His goodness, healing, and power to the end of the ages. Will you join Him? We do this by not erasing our past, but letting Jesus redeem it and then declaring it to a hungry and hurting world. As Manning puts it, "In a futile attempt to erase our past, we deprive the community of our healing gift. If we conceal our wounds out of fear and shame, our inner darkness can neither be illuminated nor become a light for others."[6]

The best way to live in the light is to not only be okay with but get excited about the fact that a perfect God wants to use your imperfect past to bring about profound healing in your life and the lives around you.

If this overwhelms you and you're slightly breaking out into a sweat at the thought of living this out like I did that night at Bible study, be encouraged, friend. We can be this for others because we have a Jesus who is this for us. Through His life, we have everything we need and more to show up, do the hard work of healing, and let God start to use us for His glory.

THE MODEL JESUS SETS FOR US IN COMMUNITY

I am so grateful that Jesus will never call us to something He hasn't already provided the framework for through His life and ministry. Everything we've been working through in this chapter about community isn't from some well-meaning, cultural rule of thumb. It's straight from Jesus. Let's dive into the Word and see how Jesus makes time for us, weeps with us, and pours out His life for us.

Jesus Makes Time for Us

First, just like Dottie, Jesus makes time for us. Time and time again, we see Jesus not just tolerate but welcome "inconvenience" from those who really need Him.

One of the hardest memories for me was the day that my dad sat me down and told me he had been diagnosed with stage-four liver cancer. I'll never forget the details of that moment. The townhouse we were living in. The look in his sick eyes. The heart-pounding shock and grief that washed over me.

After he told me the news and told me that he was going to fight to stay alive for me and my sister, I sat quietly and asked if I could excuse myself to go up to my room. I still remember the walk up the stairs to my room as it felt like I had fifty-pound dumbbells chained to my ankles.

Reaching the top of my stairs, I shut myself in my room, sat at the end of my bed, and cried. And cried. And cried. Even to this day, I had never been so stricken with grief and hopelessness. Not only that, I remember the sobering reality of feeling utterly alone.

When we think back to the hard, lonely, hopeless moments of our lives, it's hard to believe that Jesus was there. Faith to believe Jesus is in the mountaintop moments is easy. Faith to believe that Jesus is in the valley is a different story. So how are we called to see these moments of our past when it comes to the presence of Jesus?

One of my favorite examples of Jesus' heart for us comes from a moment when even His friends assumed that He was too busy for a certain group of people. "Then children were brought to him that he might lay his hands on them and pray. The disciples rebuked the people, but Jesus said, 'Let the little children come to me and do not hinder them, for to such belongs the kingdom of heaven.' And he laid his hands on them and went away" (Matt. 19:13–15).

Jesus, someone who could have easily acted preoccupied by some of the "bigger" tasks of His day, knew that these seemingly mundane moments were actually the most significant. Why? Because Jesus knew that God's children need Him. He knows that I need Him and that you do, too. Jesus was displaying the true heart of God to show us that He will always make time for us.

That same Jesus who stopped for the children that day stopped for me when I got the news that forever changed my life. The news that would lead me to adopt the false identity of an abandoned daughter for many years to come. And with all the compassion and love for that younger version of me, I wish I could tell her that her feelings weren't true.

When I felt all alone on my bed, He was there sitting on the edge with me.

When I felt like I was falling deeper and deeper into despair, He was holding me firmly in His grasp.

When I felt abandoned, He never left my side.

Jesus was right there the whole time. In my darkest moment, Jesus wasn't absent or missing. He was right in the middle of it. Present. Unrushed. Available.

This is who our God is. Just as He wouldn't let anyone get in the way of the children coming to Him, He does the same for us. Jesus will always make Himself accessible to us. Nothing can or ever will get in His way. He controls the time, and He has the time for us.

Anyone who has ever gone through a difficult season can tell you that the well-meaning phrase that "time heals" isn't true. But I will tell you what, time with Jesus definitely does.

Friend, I pray you can start to see the ways that Jesus makes time for you as well. My encouragement to you when it comes to these heavy areas that we wish would just disappear from our aching hearts would be one word: "let."

Let God show you where He was in the sadness.

Let Him show you the pace of grace that He sets for you to heal.

Let Him wrap His arms around you as your heavenly Father.

Let Him show you that you are worth making time for.

Jesus Cries with and for Us

Next, Jesus doesn't just make time to sit with us, but He cries with and for us.

As I shared, a lot of tears were shed that day that I got the news of my dad's diagnosis. It's so important that we know that Jesus is with us, but it's also crucial that we have a correct understanding of what Jesus is doing when He's with us. In our moments of pain, what's His response?

In John's gospel, we see such a vulnerable and tender moment from Jesus when He finds out that His beloved friend, Lazarus, had passed away.

Now when Mary came to where Jesus was and saw him, she fell at his feet, saying to him, "Lord, if you had been here, my brother would not have died." *When Jesus saw her weeping, and the Jews who had come with her also weeping, he was deeply moved in his spirit and greatly troubled. And he said, "Where have you laid him?" They said to him, "Lord, come and see." Jesus wept.* (John 11:32–35, emphasis added)

Knowing that Jesus indeed was God incarnate, it would have been so easy and even understandable for Jesus to save His tears, knowing that "in all things God works for the good of those who love him, who have been called according to his purpose" (Rom. 8:28). Especially given the second half of the story:

Then Jesus, deeply moved again, came to the tomb. It was a cave, and a stone lay against it. Jesus said, "Take away the stone." . . . And Jesus lifted up his eyes and said, "Father, I thank you that you have heard me. I knew that you always hear me, but I said this on account of the people standing around, that they may believe that you sent me." When he had said these things, he cried out with a loud voice, "Lazarus, come out." The man who had died came out, his hands and feet bound with linen strips, and his face wrapped with a cloth. Jesus said to them, "Unbind him, and let him go." (John 11:38–39a, 41a–44)

What a compassionate Savior we have. We see from the ending that Jesus always knew that His friend would be raised, even when no one else did. From this, we know that Jesus didn't cry out of a place of hopelessness, but He cried out of a place of empathy and love for those whose hearts are broken.

It took me a while to believe it, but I know that Jesus wasn't just sitting on the edge of the bed with me that day, He was also crying tears with me. As my fifteen-year-old self experienced pain and grief, the empathic Jesus felt and shared in that same pain. As Isaiah prophesied years prior, Jesus is "a man of sorrows and acquainted with grief" (Isa. 53:3).

The beautiful example Jesus sets for us here is that two things can be true at once. We know that a day is coming that "he will wipe away every tear from their eyes, and death shall be no more, neither shall there be mourning, nor crying, nor pain anymore, for the former things have passed away" (Rev. 21:4). This is the beautiful hope that we have because of the sacrifice of Jesus to trade his life for ours. But it doesn't wipe away pain today, it joins it. Friend, we can grieve, but not without hope. Jesus shows us how to beautifully hold the two together in perfect harmony.

Jesus doesn't just show up. He enters into our pain, full of sorrow and full of hope.

He cried with Mary. He cried with me. He sits on the end of the bed and mourns with you, too. Jesus is in the pain with us just as much as He is in the victories of our lives.

Jesus weeps with us.

Jesus Pours Out His Life for Us

Last but not least, Jesus pours out His life for us.

I often forget that Jesus could have lived His life very differently, and He would have been completely justified in it. Jesus was perfect, blameless, and worthy of all praise and glory. Yet, He chose to become lowly and the sacrificial lamb for us. Even from His first breath, He was born into lowliness and weakness. Jesus came "not to be served but to serve, and to give his life as a ransom for many" (Matt. 20:28).

I feel like God's been pointing me to verses and situations that reveal my weaknesses everywhere I turn these days. Not in a self-deprecating way, but just in a very real way. A human way. The Greek word for *weakness* is incredibly hard to translate. Almost impossible. So much so that a more accurate translation would be more like "the human condition." Whew. Talk about having to face reality.

Have you ever thought about that fact that Jesus was even sovereign over His own birth? He could have been born anywhere. But where did He choose to be born? In a stable. It was messy. It was literally where sheep went to the bathroom. And that's where He chose to enter into the world—into a messy stable and into our messy world.

The King of kings put on weakness, for you and for me. He was born into weakness and in weakness He humbled Himself to the point of dying on a cross. At His birth, He was wrapped in swaddles meant for a lamb, a helpless and weak animal. From His first breath, He was preparing Himself as the spotless lamb of God—the perfect sacrifice.

Hebrews 4:15–16 declares, "For we do not have a high priest who is unable to sympathize with our weaknesses, but one who in every respect has been tempted as we are, yet without sin. Let us then with confidence draw near to the throne of grace, that we may receive mercy and find grace to help in time of need."

I don't know about you, but weakness sounds a lot more appealing after letting that sink in. I'm a lot more prone to embrace my human condition if it means I get more of Jesus, who has poured out His life for you and for me.

We hear it all the time but let's actually begin to lay down our false confidence and pride, and with open hands, let's pray bold prayers like, "Jesus, let Your power be made perfect in my weakness. For when I am weak, then I am strong."

Jesus pours out His life for us.

THE RIGHT NEXT STEP

After that day with Dottie, it's not that I was a new person. There wasn't a magical formula that we followed to make me "free." And there definitely wasn't anything special in that poptart except for refined sugar and carbs. But through the tears, the messy conversation, and the needed silence, I was given the gift of stepping into more of *who I already was.*

That day gave me the launchpad to believe that true freedom was possible when we believe that what the enemy intends for evil, God uses for good.

We can choose to take the scary step in being known because we trust that Jesus knows and accepts us first. We pour out into our community because Jesus did the ultimate pouring out for us. We don't pour from an empty cup. We pour from a cup that overflows with the blood of the Lamb and word of our testimony (Rev. 12:11). This is what leads to our next step: true forgiveness of ourselves and others.

how to finally forgive yourself

There is a sentence that every girl with a past dreads hearing: *We need to talk about our pasts.*

As Ryan and I were getting more serious and moving toward marriage, the excitement that God might have led me to my husband was at an all-time high. This also came with a fear and heaviness regarding the conversations you should have before entering marriage. I knew that I didn't want to go into marriage with anything hidden or kept in the dark. If we wanted a healthy marriage, all things had to come to the light.

One of the biggest areas of shame for me was my sexual past prior to fully surrendering my life to Jesus. As we talked about earlier, God has such a good design for intimacy within marriage. Although intellectually I knew I had been forgiven and redeemed through Jesus, I feared that the facts of my looming past might be too much for Ryan.

Sharing our past with anyone is hard. It's personal. It's vulnerable. It's scary. And at the time, it was becoming my reality. Yes, I had talked with my friend, Dottie, and received such grace and freedom from that experience, but this felt like a whole other monster.

God, You want me to share with my future husband—the man I'm going to be intimate with for the rest of my life—how many other guys I've been with? And I'm supposed to trust that he will also forgive me and see me through the lens of forgiveness? Are you sure?

The shame still lingered in a way that the thought alone of having these difficult conversations gave me a pit in my stomach, and it seemed as though it was a losing battle.

In times like these, I found it so helpful to cling to this truth: "'Come now, let us settle the matter,' says the LORD. 'Though your sins are like scarlet, they shall be as white as snow; though they are red as crimson, they shall be like wool'" (Isa. 1:18 NIV). As well as: "For I will be merciful toward their iniquities, and I will remember their sins no more" (Heb. 8:12).

At the end of the day, I knew hearing some of the things I was going to share would be hard on Ryan. After all, he had fallen in love with me. He treasured me. He had a healthy protective nature over me, and it wasn't going to be easy to digest some of the life I had lived before I met him. As I prepared and processed, I realized it would be just as hard for me to actually say it all out loud.

I wish I could share that I went into our conversation confident and living out of the truth that God remembered my sins no more and I was now deemed white as snow because of Jesus. I wish I could tell you that I was confident that Ryan would look at me and say what everyone thinks a perfect guy should say: "Morgan, that was then. This is now. You have been covered by the blood of Jesus. We are all in need of forgiveness, and my sin is just as heavy as yours, even if not on paper. I completely forgive you." Instead, I was terrified.

I knew that Ryan believed the truth above, but I also knew he was a human who was going to have to bring this to the Lord and wrestle with his own struggle to forgive.

"THE TALK"

Relationships are messy. Forgiveness isn't always immediate in the human heart, even when Jesus is at the center of a relationship. However, there we were, two sinners saved by grace dedicated to doing the hard work. Yes, for our relationship, but even more importantly, for our own sanctification and redemption stories.

> Forgiveness isn't always immediate in the human heart, even when Jesus is at the center of a relationship.

So on a weeknight in August, Ryan and I got together and geared up for one of the hardest conversations of our lives.

We prayed over the pizza we were about to eat, but we both knew the prayer was more for the hard conversation ahead than for God to "bless this food to the nourishment of our bodies to His service." After the prayer, we dove into the pizza and into the hard.

Like the gentleman he is, Ryan graciously went first. He shared his past struggles and sought forgiveness from me. Again, I believe that all sin is equal and there are no "darker" sins in God's eyes. But the truth is, Ryan's struggles at the time just didn't seem as shameful as mine. In full transparency, Ryan had saved himself for marriage. I hadn't. As grateful as I was to know that I would be his one and only, it also terrified me all the more knowing what I had to share.

It came time for me to take the hotseat. What came next wasn't pretty. I was quickly slumped over in my chair, my head as low as it could go, and tears streaming down my face (accompanied by snot). Before I knew it, I was on the brink of a panic attack.

Specifically, I knew God was calling me to share with Ryan the number of people I had slept with, which was a really hard subject for me. Because until Dottie, I had never even said the number out loud.

There was a time when I thought that maybe God wouldn't make me get that detailed with Ryan. I thought that maybe, just maybe, Ryan and God would be satisfied with me sharing that I had been with guys outside of marriage, and we could all three agree to leave it at that. But as we are learning, God wants to redeem every situation, every number, and every space that we will let Him into. He will redeem us in detailed ways according to how detailed we're willing to get with Him and others.

With each tear that fell, I felt more and more broken. *Why, God? Why are you making me go through this?* I thought as I sat there silent for what seemed like five hours.

I felt like the woman caught in adultery that we read about in chapter seven. Head down. Caught in her shame. Exposed. Hopeless. Fearful.

Through my heavy, exasperated breaths, I finally uttered the details that had been weighing on me for so long.

And I immediately stopped crying, felt freed, and we moved on after hugging and breaking out into song! I'm kidding. It was not that pretty. The truth is, my tears broke into a whole monsoon as I had reached the peak of my exposure and vulnerability. I had no idea what would happen next. So I sat there, with my head down, unsure what could possibly follow this heavy moment.

Through my blurry vision, I saw Ryan's hands, palms up, reaching out to me. Not just reaching out, but openhandedly inviting me to grab onto him. The symbolism was unmistakable. To me, it communicated that yes, this is hard, but I will forgive you, and I am in this with you. But in that moment, I felt so paralyzed that I was unable to meet him in that space. I never reached out and grabbed his hands.

There was no pretty bow on this night, just lots of tears shed by us both.

The untied bow of that hard night showed me something: as exposed as I felt that night, what was more exposed to me was how long Jesus had been reaching out His hands to me, palms open and nail-scarred, offering me total forgiveness. Up until that point, I thought I had received it. But I realized in that moment that I hadn't, at least not in the fullness and depth that it was being offered to me.

> We will never be able to **receive forgiveness from others** until we receive it from the One who created forgiveness.

Through this, I learned that *I would never be able to receive forgiveness from Ryan or anyone else until I received it from the One who created forgiveness.* Friend, until you and I are willing to face our wounds and the depths of our sin and bring it to the Jesus who proclaims, "It is finished," we will not be able to move forward in our freedom journeys.

WHY WE STRUGGLE TO RECEIVE FORGIVENESS

As I reflected on the night and why I was unable to reach out and grab Ryan's hands, and why I had also never received the open hands of forgiveness that were offered to me in Christ, there were three main reasons. Three lies that I think so many of us get stuck in when it comes to past shame, rendering us unable to receive forgiveness.

Reason #1: It's Easier to Punish Ourselves than to Receive Grace

Let's be honest. Grace is uncomfortable. In a world that hangs its hat on the "hustle," making a name for ourselves, and the mentality that "you eat what you kill," grace is completely contradictory to our natural wiring. Our cultural wiring is simple:

Succeed = celebrate yourself.

Fail = punish yourself.

Unfortunately, what we find when we plug ourselves into the world's formula, the one who ends up suffering the most is us. Not others. Not God. Us.

If you're anything like me, you may do this strange thing when you blow it. We decide to distance ourself from those we may have hurt, even if they respond to us with grace, compassion, and forgiveness.

For example, there have been seasons of my life where I have been a good friend, and times where I could have been better. If I'm honest, sometimes I can get so caught up in my own world and to-do list that I neglect the relationships that I value most. A forgotten birthday. A failure to return the call. A lack of following up on something a friend shared that they're walking through. Whatever it might be, once it catches up with me and I stop to reflect, I feel like a really bad friend. In these moments, my natural tendency is to pull away and avoid them all the more, almost as a way of self-punishment. But time after time, I have been met with that uncomfortable grace that is completely un-merited. The truth is, receiving this type of kindness when we've blown it feels uncomfortable. It's hard to receive. It's undeserved.

I can't help but think how this echoes the cries of our Father in moments when we refuse to receive the gift of grace in our lowest of lows.

We have a God who longs for us. He desires to be near us. He's eager for us to encounter Him. He's jealous for more time with us. When we punish ourselves, we refuse His invitation to commune with us.

You may think the only way to make yourself feel better is self-condemnation, but the true remedy in moments of shame is to run to the Father who sent His Son to die for this very reason.

Like I said, grace is uncomfortable. It feels messy. It feels unbalanced. That's because it is. I'm not going to lie. There are times when I hate that I can't do anything to earn forgiveness. I crave to do something that merits me the grace that's offered to me day by day, moment by moment. But in these moments, we must remind ourselves of the confident trust we find in Paul's letter to the church in Ephesus: "For by grace you have been saved through faith. And this is not your own doing; it is the gift of God, not a result of works, so that no one may boast. For we are his workmanship, created in Christ Jesus for good works, which God prepared beforehand, that we should walk in them" (Eph. 2:8–10).

> Jesus is grace. Grace is Jesus. Trade your fig leaves of self-condemnation for the free grace found on the cross.

Have you ever taken a step toward uncomfortable grace? Have you really sat in this unmerited gift that is fully available, fully yours in Christ?

No time of punishment, no self-condemnation, no distance from God will ever grant you earned grace. It just doesn't exist. I'd like to argue that without receiving *this* grace, you can't really receive Jesus. They go hand in hand. Jesus *is* grace. Grace *is* Jesus. Trade your fig leaves of self-condemnation for the free grace found on the cross.

Grace bids us come even when it feels unnatural. Especially when it feels unnatural. What if today you take hold of the open hands that Jesus holds out in your direction?

Reason #2: We Have a Small View of the Work on the Cross

We know we need to receive grace, but why does it seem so unrealistic to receive and start to live out of it? It is because of our small view of the place where grace became available to us: the cross.

I don't know about you, but I see a lot of tiny crosses over big crosses these days.

I see tiny crosses around necks.

I see tiny crosses on people's wrists.

I see tiny crosses woven into companies' logos.

And don't get me wrong, there is absolutely nothing wrong with this. But over time, just like these tiny crosses, our views of the significance of the cross becomes . . . tiny.

I'll never forget one of the most memorable car rides I've ever had. Two of my friends and I were heading back from Louisiana after being a part of a birthday weekend turned marriage proposal. (So special!) As we drove home, we somehow ended up taking the long way back by accident and found ourselves surrounded by nothing but farmland and tractors that made us feel like we were on the set of the movie *Transformers*. We were perplexed and a bit frustrated that it was going to take us an extra two hours to get home. But it opened up the space and time to have a real conversation about how we were doing on a heart level.

Isn't it interesting that God will take you the long way sometimes to put you right where He wants you? Another chapter for another book.

One of my friends, when asked how she was doing, didn't hold back. She said she was having a really hard time due to a few factors and was in a spiritual rut that was affecting her as a wife, mother, and friend.

We encouraged her in that moment, and God really put it on my heart to share with her how much He was near and pursuing her, even if she didn't feel it.

Right as we were sharing, on a completely open and empty road, we were stopped by a construction worker holding a "STOP" sign. We laughed at the irony as we didn't really see a need to stop right there in the middle of nowhere, but we complied, stopped the car, and rolled down the window.

The man asked us where we were heading, and we told him back to Nashville. With a soft smile and a nod of his head, he looked my friend square in the eye and said, "I hope you find your way."

As we drove away, we couldn't help but sense the significance of that moment, especially for my friend. She was impacted and touched by the man's words. It was as if God put him right there for her, displaying a tiny glimpse of His vast pursuit of her.

What followed was purely God showing off. It was like everything on that car ride pointed to Jesus. A song on the radio about the Father's love. A billboard with John 3:16, and finally, three massive crosses off to the left that, when my friend laid eyes on, she became speechless.

It was the sweetest day hearing my friend point out all the ways she was seeing God pour Himself out to her that day.

With every display, she would scream out like a little girl in a theme park, *"Did you hear that lyric?" "Do you see that billboard?" "Oh my goodness, guys, look at those crosses!"*

It was beautiful. It was how it should be.

You see, those crosses, that song, and the billboard were all already there. God didn't magically build it into that very moment. It already existed before we hit the road that day. But the difference is that my friend had the ears to hear and the eyes to see the love of God that was all around her. The same love that is right in front of you and me today.

> There is nothing Jesus won't do **to redeem and reconcile** us to Himself.

When it comes to the cross, so many of us struggle to live as forgiven daughters because our eyes aren't seeing the vastness of all that it truly is.

As we talked about in the last chapter, just as Jesus was sovereign over His own birth, He was also sovereign over His own death. Have you ever thought about that? Jesus—Creator and King of the universe—had complete control over how and when He would come and die.

What did He choose? Jesus chose to enter into a time where the severity of the death penalty was at an all-time high: crucifixion.

Why did He do this? I believe one reason He did it was to show us that there is nothing He won't do to redeem and reconcile us to Himself.

The cross isn't just a symbol of a big death. It's the symbol of a big love. A love that years before was prophesied by Isaiah: "He was pierced for our transgressions, he was crushed for our iniquities; the punishment that brought us peace was on him, and by his wounds we are healed" (Isa. 53:5 NIV).

Because see, we need a big love. We need healing because we are wounded people. Often, our view of the cross is measured by our view of our sin. If we view our sin as small, the cross will always be small.

I once saw a visual of this drawn out that gave this truth new life in my heart.

There were two lines. One line going down and one line going up. The line going down represents our understanding of our sin, and the line going up represents grace. As we grasp the true depth of our sin, the line goes deeper and deeper down. And as we see our sin more clearly, the above line of grace goes up and up and up.

The space in between is where the cross meets up. And the more we grow in our understanding of sin and grace, what does the cross do? It grows. Bigger and bigger and bigger. All of a sudden, our view of the cross grows to insurmountable heights.

What Jesus accomplished for us on the cross is bigger than any of us will ever be able to truly comprehend. The invitation of Jesus is to safely bring our sin to Him, be met with grace, and trade our tiny crosses and fig leaves for the cross. The cross that hung our Savior who died, resurrected, and defeated death once and for all. Through this, He finally proved the words He spoke with His depleted last breath: "Father, forgive them, for they know not what they do" (Luke 23:34).

Whether we see it or not, the cross is a big one. Our Savior is not the junior varsity version we try to make Him. Our call is to see Him as He is and to trust that the work He accomplished for us is enough for us to walk as daughters of redemption.

Reason #3: We Don't Believe God Can Actually Redeem Our Wounds

After Ryan and I had our conversation over pizza (that inevitably turned very cold by the end of our time together), I realized that it was going to take a true miracle for me to receive the forgiveness that I said I believed in. On top of that, I remember whispering a prayer, "God, don't just teach about forgiveness through this. Teach me about your power of redemption."

I was starting to realize something absolutely crucial to one's journey to freedom from shame: You can receive forgiveness from your past and still be waiting for moments of redemption. Forgiveness is immediate, but in God's kindness, redemption of certain details of your story is a progression. Redemption is the process of Jesus taking you back to the painful, broken, and shame-filled moments of your past, showing you where He was in it, and turning it for good in a way that only He can. These moments of redemption and the freedom that goes with it come when you begin to believe and accept your true identity as a forgiven, precious daughter of the God who created you.

I believe you can't reduce the workings of God in your life to a

> Redemption is the process of Jesus taking you back to the painful, broken, and shame-filled moments of your past, **showing you where He was in it,** and turning it for good in a way that only He can.

formula. But for the sake of explaining this, here is a way to see the progression of how God wants to bring us to a place of true freedom.

Repentance + Receive Forgiveness + Believe in Redemption = WALK IN FREEDOM.

I didn't want to just stop at forgiveness. I was hungry for God to redeem me in a way that was so far beyond anything I could ever do. After all, we can't erase the past. What's happened to us or been done by us, unfortunately, isn't going to magically disappear. But even better, God can take the brokenness from the past and do something so beautiful, so redemptive, and so supernatural that our greatest shame now becomes our greatest testimony.

I wanted that.

That was truly the first time I took this Scripture seriously: "to grant to those who mourn in Zion—to give them a beautiful headdress instead of ashes, the oil of gladness instead of mourning, the garment of praise instead of a faint spirit; that they may be called oaks of righteousness, the planting of the LORD, that he may be glorified" (Isa. 61:3).

> Without our wounds, we will never have any reason to collapse into the One who truly heals.

If I was going to give my past over to Jesus, I wanted Him to do something with it. I wanted a story I could tell for His glory. I wanted the kind of redemption that points people to the miracle-working God who truly trades beauty for ashes.

As the weeks passed, Ryan and I didn't seek comfort or security from one another. We dedicated ourselves to seeking those things from the only One who gives them. I spent a *lot* more time with Jesus and a *lot* less time with Ryan in the month following. I needed to hear Jesus' voice and knew that Ryan's forgiveness of me would only come secondary to receiving it from Jesus.

Jesus taught me a lot about wounds in that month. For the first time, I was starting to really see my wounds as a gift. Without our wounds, we will never have any reason to collapse into the One who truly heals.

I was starting to embrace my wounds.

I was starting to seek healing for my wounds.

I was beginning to pray bold prayers, believing that Jesus could heal my wounds for His glory.

What came next was an answer to that prayer.

About a month after our conversation, Ryan and I were in the car heading to a friend's house. We hadn't talked about the details of our previous conversation much, but we were trusting that we were both seeking the Lord for answers on how to move forward.

As a surprise to me, he brought it up and said he wanted to follow up.

I was nervous, but one thing I always trusted was Ryan's relationship with Jesus. So in that moment, I chose to trust not just Ryan, but also Jesus that He was in this.

Ryan explained to me that he had really been bringing our conversation to God and a few trusted mentors in his life and was fighting to reconcile the past so we could move forward in our life together.

Then he said something I'll never forget: "Morgan, I know how hard that was for you to share with me the details of your past. I've been seeking the Lord on how to view all of this, and He's been gently reminding me that because of Jesus, both of us are made new. The old is gone. He's paid for both of our pasts on the cross. And I believe God is going to use our testimony of redemtion for years to come. I love you."

I was speechless. In an instant, God put on display what I've been trying to communicate throughout this entire book: *Jesus can and will redeem any area that you will let Him into.*

I was overcome with the oceanic, undeserved grace. It flooded into every doubt, fear, or area of shame inside of me at that moment.

So many of us fall into the trap of believing that it's "finally finding the one" that completes us. We look horizontally to find ultimate fulfillment when we were created to look vertically.

> Jesus **can and will redeem** any area that you will let Him into.

I know we didn't walk the earth in Jesus' day, but if you think about it, you can't look to the cross without looking vertically. You can only behold the beauty of the cross by looking up.

That day, it wasn't Ryan who was completing me or making me whole, it was Jesus.

See, the good work that He starts will always be completed. God doesn't leave things undone. We leave a lot of things incomplete—a project, a puzzle, a space we want to organize, laundry, conversations—but God never does.

Theologian Charles Spurgeon argued, "Where is there an instance of God's beginning any work and leaving it incomplete? Show me for once a world abandoned and thrown aside half formed; show me a universe cast off from the Great Potter's wheel, with the design in outline, the clay half hardened, and the form unshapely from incompleteness."[1]

This promise is laced throughout Scripture. He is a God who completes.

The apostle Paul started his letter to the church in Philippi with this assurance: "I am sure of this, that he who began a good work in you will bring it to completion at the day of Jesus Christ" (Phil. 1:6).

Friend, that good work is you. That promise is for you. The completion is yours in Christ.

It would be easy to read these pages and think to yourself, *God can't redeem my life and my story like that. If only you knew what I've been through, Morgan. It's too dark, too messy, too far gone.*

Chances are, God won't do the exact same thing in your story as mine. Your redemption and completeness won't come like mine. It will be even better because it will be meant specifically for you—that is, if you're willing to let Him into that difficult, painful wound you've been holding on to.

Trust me, Jesus knows a thing or two about wounds. But Jesus has the antidote: Himself.

By whose wounds are we healed? *His wounds* (Isa. 53:5).

As Dane Ortlund puts it, "Your suffering does not define you. His does."[2]

It's His suffering on the cross, His completion, that we cling to.

I was beyond grateful and changed by the revelation God laid on Ryan's heart that day, but the true healing and redemption came when I set my gaze on the true object of my healing, the healer Himself.

Friend, we might not experience total completeness and healing on this side of heaven. But that doesn't mean God will not enter into the dark corners of your past and do a good work starting today that *He* will bring to completion on the day of Christ's return.

Just as the phrase "we need to talk about our past" hung over me, the grace of Christ redeemed me. Regardless of your story, the power in the complete work of the cross is available to you right now in this moment and forevermore. You don't need a husband for that.

Friend, what needs forgiveness in your life? And what lies are you believing that might be holding you back from receiving what has already been purchased for you? Maybe today is the day to finally let Jesus into those moments and allow Him to show you His take on the situation. As scary as it feels, if you decide to let Him in, I have a feeling He will be right there, full of compassion and with an eagerness of heart to do a good work in this area. Finally forgiving yourself means letting Jesus in and allowing Him to show you His heart and plan for forgiveness.

He will forgive.

He will heal.

He will free.

He will redeem.

PART 4

walking in
freedom

why wholeness is better than perfection

We've covered a lot so far, but I want you to clear your mind for a moment. Think back to a time. Maybe it was yesterday, last week, five years ago, when you were five—think about a time you felt truly alive. A time you felt whole. Don't overcomplicate it. Think about where you were. Think about who you were with. What were you doing? What were you thinking about? What were you *not* thinking about? What were you not worried or anxious about that you might be in this season? How present were you?

Friend, whatever that moment was for you, I want you to realize the holiness of that moment in time. I want you to see that the state you were in—that's God's heart for you. Not the anxiousness and half-heartedness you might find yourself

> If we want to be wholehearted, we have to know and truly understand the Father's heart.

in. It doesn't mean all our moments will be like that one. But the beauty of a life lived with Jesus is that there is a peace that surpasses our circumstances and our past. Our wholeness of heart can transcend the brokenness we've walked through.

Paul says in Philippians that he has learned the key to being content, or "whole," in all circumstances:

Not that I am speaking of being in need, for I have learned in whatever situation I am to be content. I know how to be brought low, and I know how to abound. In any and every circumstance, I have learned the secret of facing plenty and hunger, abundance and need. I can do all things through him who strengthens me. (Phil. 4:11–13)

I think for too long, we have been letting our circumstances determine how we live as wholehearted, forgiven daughters. This is not God's heart for us. If we want to be wholehearted, we have to know and truly understand the Father's heart.

EXACTLY WHAT YOU NEED

As we've discovered in these pages, everything changes when we know the Father's heart for us. Besides the life of Jesus, there is no better picture of this that we get in Scripture than in the relationship between King David and his son, Solomon.

Most of you know King David. He was the appointed king of Israel from the tribe of Judah. He was an unassuming shepherd who God chose to use in mighty ways. In humility toward God, he accomplished great things in his life. Check it out:

- A humble leader. From his story, we get the phrase, "Man looks on the outward appearance, but the LORD looks on the heart" (1 Sam. 16:7).
- A fierce warrior. To the point that he had songs sung about him in battle.
- He killed Goliath. Enough said.

- He escaped death countless times and then extended mercy to those who tried to kill him.
- He is the writer of most of the Psalms (think *NYT* bestselling author and top Christian album on Apple . . . no big deal).

And don't get me wrong, David also had a past (relatable). He lived with a past that had "murderer" and "adulterer" on his résumé, but still, God saw David as a "man after his own heart" (1 Sam. 13:14). If anything, David's life points to the goodness of the unconditional love of the Father.

This relationship led to the Lord making a covenant with David stating that he *was* the rightful king of Israel and that his throne would be established forever.

David had many children, one of them being Solomon.

One of the greatest tasks of David's life was to prepare a temple to be made for the Lord's presence. He was old, so God charged Solomon to build it.

As a good father, David knew that he had to prepare everything for Solomon to be able to pull this thing off. "David said, 'My son Solomon is young and inexperienced, and the house to be built for the LORD should be of great magnificence and fame and splendor in the sight of all the nations. Therefore I will make preparations for it.' So David made extensive preparations before his death" (1 Chron. 22:5 NIV). He prepared every stone, all gold, silver, bronze, iron, all positions, musicians, gatekeepers (security), treasurers, military, and every other thing he would need.

(Maybe you need to hear today that the Father prepares for you exactly what you'll need. Just as we learned in chapter one, God will always go before us.)

King David did it *all*.

And at the very end of his life, he gave a monumental speech and prayer to the people of Israel and specifically to his son.

If you've ever seen someone at the end of their life, you know that they use their words wisely. We should all pay attention to this charge. He prayed this prayer for his son and God's people:

"O LORD our God, all this abundance that we have provided for building you a house for your holy name comes from your hand and is all your own. I know, my God, that you test the heart and have pleasure in uprightness. In the uprightness of my heart I have freely offered all these things, and now I have seen your people, who are present here, offering freely and joyously to you. O LORD, the God of Abraham, Isaac, and Israel, our fathers, keep forever such purposes and thoughts in the hearts of your people, and direct their hearts toward you. Grant to Solomon my son a *whole heart* that he may keep your commandments, your testimonies, and your statutes, performing all, and that he may build the palace for which I have made provision." (1 Chron. 29:16–19, emphasis added)

What a beautiful prayer. David didn't pray that God would make his son rich, established, or successful, but *wholly* sincere and dedicated to God. That's the good news—that we have a God who just asks us to be whole. Not perfect, but whole. See, there's a difference. When we think of something being "whole," we think it's perfect and that the work is done. The truth is, you can be a work in progress and still live a life of wholeheartedness, flaws and all.

Perfection is about achievement.

Wholeness is about giving what you have.

Perfection is all about the end result.

Wholeness is about the journey.

Perfection is about pride.

Wholeness is about humility.

A JOURNEY, NOT A DESTINATION

One of my favorite verses when I think about this journey we're on to freedom, redemption, and wholeness comes from Paul to the church in Corinth: "And we all, with unveiled face, beholding the glory of the Lord, are being transformed into the same image from one degree of glory to another. For this comes from the Lord who is the Spirit" (2 Cor. 3:18).

From one degree of glory to another. A journey, not a destination. Not that we don't have a destination. We do. Heaven is our home. But on earth, God is so much more concerned with us as broken vessels,

> As long as we are on this side of heaven, **God is still in the business of redeeming**, piece by piece, layer by layer.

not obtaining perfection, but instead returning to Him, time and time again, with a greater understanding of our desperate need for Him. And with a cry of the heart that sings the words of this famous hymn: "I need Thee ev'ry hour, teach me Thy will; and Thy rich promises in me fulfill."[1]

Because as long as we are on this side of heaven, God is still in the business of redeeming, piece by piece, layer by layer. That's the walk of a follower of Jesus. *It's the gentle, daily revelation of the deep love of a Father that is always healing our wounds from our past.*

When I think on my own story of redemption, I think back to the journey of my husband and I conceiving our first child.

I know that some people have tried to have children for years and years, and there are plenty of stories out there of couples who were never able to conceive. I never want to make light of that or compare our story to theirs.

But within our story, we tried for eighteen months to get pregnant. It was hard. It stretched us in areas we didn't expect and grew our faith in such significant ways. It brought us closer and, looking back, I can see how much purpose that season had.

I can't fully explain why, but there was a sense of shame that I was hit with after about six months of "not being able to" conceive. People hear how long you've been trying, and with great intentions, everyone tries to give their advice and recommendations on how to make it happen. It always left me feeling ashamed that it was taking so long.

Along the way, there were moments when I felt tempted to take matters into my own hands. But each time, I felt deep in my spirit that God wanted to do something in me before He placed a baby inside me. Almost like He wanted to prepare me to carry such a beautiful miracle. But it didn't take the struggle of shame away.

There were questions deep in my spirit like, *Is this what I deserve for neglecting my body in the past?* Or, *Is something wrong with me?*

After about a year of trying, something resurfaced in my mind about my past that I had forgotten was there. I think sometimes we suppress things so deeply that we forget they happened. But the season of desiring to have a baby was the perfect opportunity for the enemy to dig up the past. But remember, any time the enemy wants us to relive the past, *Jesus is always nearby with a forceful pursuit to redeem it.*

As my understanding of the miracle of life grew and grew along with the desire to become a mama, the daunting reality of decisions I had made in my past became impossible to ignore.

When I was in high school and college, I wasn't walking with Jesus. With that, I didn't value human life or see it through the lens of human beings created in the image of God. Because of that, there were nights when, out of concern, selfishness, and fear, I took the "morning-after pill."

At the time, apart from Christ, I could come up with every justification in the book to take that pill.

"Just to be safe," I said.

"We wouldn't be ready to be parents," I justified.

"I'd feel better not taking the risk," I argued.

Years later, while trying to have a baby and seeing the value of life in the womb, I was absolutely devastated at what I had done. Human life is of the greatest value over anything else on earth. And here I was, wanting a baby now and knowing the decisions I made in my past to take matters into my own hands. It broke my heart. Even worse, the reality that I'll never know if I would have conceived was a lot to carry. It still is in moments.

> Anytime the enemy wants to relive the past, Jesus is always nearby with a forceful pursuit to redeem it.

"Where do I go from here, God?" my soul cried out. I felt the reassurance of what has been the entire theme of my life (and yours, too, even if you can't see it): *God redeems*. He takes the darkest situation and works miracles in the middle of those areas. Not through demanding perfection, but through making us something that, apart from Him, is truly impossible: *whole*.

FIGHTING THE WHOLEHEARTED FIGHT

David didn't need his son to be perfect. He just needed Solomon to give all he had, knowing that God would sustain him. Knowing that the good work God had begun in him, *God* would bring it to completion.

Hopefully, right about now, if you appreciate a good story, you're asking the question, "Well . . . did he? Did Solomon remain wholehearted?"

Here's the bad news . . . no, he did not. He did for a while, but he didn't stay dedicated to the one hope that God had for him. It's really fascinating because three main factors drew him away from whole-heartedness, and I believe God wants us to be aware of them as we seek redemption and wholeness in our own stories.

Let's break this down together.

1. Solomon Loved the Things of the World More than the Things of God

Solomon did what was commanded of him. He built the temple. He asked for wisdom. Things seemed to be going well. The people were happy. But then there's a shift.

Because God blessed Solomon's reign, the riches and honor came flooding in. With that, Solomon shifted from worshiping God to allowing others, and eventually himself, to become the object of his worship.

He loved that people came to him for wisdom—the wisdom given to him by God (1 Kings 10:24).

He broke God's command to the people of Israel that a king must not multiply wealth for himself in the form of silver, gold, or horses (Deut. 17:14–20; 1 Kings 10:14, 26).

It seemed that Solomon would rather have everyone view him as perfect than living out of a place of wholeness. Because, as we learned, wholeness requires humility. It demands that we put down the false facade that we have it all together and, instead, run to the cross daily for our justification. Wholeness acknowledges the fact that apart from Jesus, we are nothing. We have nothing. We gain nothing. He is what fills us, not our best efforts. Our best efforts are but "filthy rags" to Him (Isa. 64:6 NIV).

We must fall in love with Jesus and live our lives to serve Him and be formed by Him, something the world will never fulfill.

2. Solomon Let the Wrong Voices Be the Loudest Voices

Over time, Solomon acquired many foreign wives who worshiped other gods. These women—the closest voices to him—became the loudest voices in his life (1 Kings 11:1–4).

Before you think this isn't relatable, don't underestimate the power of even one relationship having a huge impact on your wholehearted-ness. Some of you might not have even one husband, but you follow more than one hundred people on social media, right? You're letting each of those voices speak things and ideas into your life without even knowing it.

The voices we let into our lives will either lead us to or away from intimacy with God.

When it came to me making certain choices in my past, I listened to what the world considered "acceptable," or even worse, I listened to my own "truth" and justified my actions based on what I thought was okay in my own eyes.

During those months of having to pray and process through my past decisions to take the morning-after pill, I prayed that God would give me the *clarity and courage* to take the steps needed to receive heal-ing, forgiveness, and freedom. A huge part of this would be taking the brave step of sharing it with Ryan as well. I didn't fear his response, but I knew it would be hard for me to say. But with anything God wants to redeem in life, I knew His guiding voice would lead me to something beautiful out of the darkness if I entrusted it to Him.

3. Solomon Filled the Wrong Temple

Solomon thought he was wholeheartedly serving the Lord by building the temple as He asked. And he did to an extent. But why do you think that God wanted the temple in the first place? *So He could be with us.* So He could fill us with His love and presence.

In the Old Testament days before Jesus, the temple was God's way to be with us. To dwell among us. And Solomon missed it. He was so caught up in doing, achieving, and completing that he left vacant the main thing God wanted to fill, which was himself.

> **God wants us.** Anything He asks us to do will only be a means to an end to bring us to Him.

Friend, God wants us. Anything He asks us to do will only be a means to an end to bring us to Him.

David asked Solomon to be whole—to have an "undivided" heart—to build the temple. But really it was never fully about the building. God wanted to fill a different empty space.

Maybe today, as you read this, there are idols, spaces, or past decisions that need redemption. If so, God is near and loves doing the impossible.

So Solomon's life ends with bondage to idolatry and a love for the world over God (1 Kings 11:6).

I know this feels discouraging because we love a happy ending.

But praise be to God, *there is one.*

JESUS, THE TRUE FULFILLMENT

Solomon turned out not to be the golden child of David, but God the Father was faithful. So much so that when Jesus puts on flesh to enter into the cosmos, He is called the "Son of David" (Matt. 12:23).

See, Jesus was wholeheartedly devoted to the things of God. Jesus lived a perfect life. Even when met with the temptation of worldly status, He rejected it by becoming a humble servant.

When the wrong voices tried to speak into His life, He retreated to let God be the loudest voice.

When everyone around Him was trying to earn salvation through works, He purchased that salvation by pouring out His blood for us.

In Solomon, we see failure. In Jesus, we see fulfillment.

This *is* the Father's love on display.

For you and me, our lives will never be measured by our successes or failures. It all hangs on the achievement of the Son's accomplishment for us on the cross. In His perfection, we find our wholeness.

This was really good news for me when it came to the season of begging God to redeem my decision to take the morning-after pill and to bring me into motherhood, forgiven, freed, and whole.

As we are learning throughout this book, I knew that Jesus had forgiven me, but that he also had plans to redeem me. Or as Joseph declares in Genesis after God redeemed the years of heartache, pain, and brokenness, "As for you, you meant evil against me, but God meant it for good" (Gen. 50:20a). This is freedom—believing that God can make things good, *has plans* to make things good, and *surely will* make things good.

Around this time, I remember praying to God and asking Him to have His way when it came to how to handle these hard memories. And as a Father does, God just began pouring out His love on me. I would open Scripture and my readings for that day would be laced with truths about His redeeming grace, His love for us, and stories like Joseph's that show His good plans. On top of all of that, I became keenly aware of God's creation and the ways He pours out His love for us through it.

One example is that red birds started to pop up *everywhere* I went. Let me just tell you, I am *not* the person to notice birds. I'm not that person that's keenly aware of the specifics of nature around me. So for me, this was a rare thing to notice.

We see all throughout Scripture, God uses and accesses any part of creation that He might see fit to point to His glory. The theological term for this is *general revelation*. Psalm 19:1 says that the skies proclaim the work of God's hands. Romans 1:20 says that since creation, God's invisible qualities are on display in the world around us.

Unfortunately, we live in a culture of disbelief that often idolizes "signs" from God as proof that He is real. Even when Jesus walked the earth, the Pharisees and even His disciples often asked for a sign and Jesus rebuked this way of thinking. This is not what God intended for how creation points us back to Him. God calls us to a live by faith, not by sight (2 Cor. 5:7). However, when we walk with Him by faith, won't we have eyes to see the way a sovereign, immanent God might use the world around us to remind us that He is indeed with us? To the best of my ability, that is what I sensed God doing in my life with these red birds as I was daily seeking Him through prayer and His Word.

> Hope is **the best way** to combat shame.

I have a mentor who, years prior, told me that she was seeing red birds often in a season when she was praying for God to have His way in her heart. I happened to remember that, and so I reached out to her to ask her to remind me what they meant to her and how I should see these little new friends in my daily life. She told me that while God can use His creation for any purpose He wants, they can mean different things to different people. For her, they represented hope.

Hope is known as "to cherish a desire with anticipation: to want something to happen or be true."[2] Hope, a cherished desire. Hope, an anticipation that God can do the impossible. Hope . . . I sure needed some of that.

Paul encourages the church in Rome (and us today) that hope is the best way to combat shame: "Not only so, but we also glory in our sufferings, because we know that suffering produces perseverance; perseverance, character; and character, hope. *And hope does not put us to shame,* because God's love has been poured out into our hearts through the Holy Spirit, who has been given to us" (Rom. 5:3–5 NIV, emphasis added).

In regard to the redemption of our past, hope is going to provide the fuel for us to live with a holy expectation that God will work on our behalf to take the broken pieces of our lives and put them back together. To make them whole.

That day, I decided I was putting my hope in God that He would restore my past and neglect of human life. And by His grace, forgive me. Not just forgive me, but redeem me and make me a mother.

So how do we live a wholehearted life?

You see, the first thing to ever be said about Solomon in Scripture was that he was loved from the start (2 Sam. 12:24).

So today, know that you're loved. Know that God wants to be the ultimate provider for you. If He sent us Jesus, won't He give us every little thing that we'll need? Just like Solomon, won't God our Father provide (Matt. 6:27–31)?

That's what He did for me and what He wants to do for you. He provided in ways I could have never even dreamed.

FROM THE INSIDE OUT

After a few months of praying over this specific area of my past and daily surrendering it to Him, I could sense that Jesus was healing me from the inside out.

He was gently reminding me that my lack of conceiving up until that point was not out of punishment, but out of a place of wanting me to be whole going into motherhood.

I was receiving forgiveness from Jesus first. Then there came a shift to where I knew the time was approaching for me to let Ryan into this part of my past that I had forgotten for so many years. I never meant to hide it from him, but it was a deep wound that I truly tried to forget.

At the perfect time, Jesus was calling me to bring it to the light and trust Him with the outcome.

So one Saturday morning in the spring, Ryan and I were sitting on two parallel couches in our living room as we individually spent time with Jesus while sipping our coffees. It was at that moment that I felt Jesus telling me it was time to share this part of my past. He had done the healing work within, and now it was time to take the next step of redemption and tell my husband about this area of my life and how it had been weighing on me. I needed to confess how I was wrestling with the lie that my past was causing the inability to conceive a child.

As my heart started pounding, I looked up from my Bible and into the large window in the front of our house. And, of course, I saw none other than a beautiful red bird perched right in front of me. And in that moment, I was reminded once again that *hope does not put us to shame.*

Taking a deep inhale, I turned toward Ryan and asked if I could share something with him. I shared it all. I shared about taking the morning-after pill. I shared my struggle to believe that I had blown it. I shared all that Jesus had been doing in my heart to bring me to that point.

Ryan didn't hesitate to join me on the couch I was on, and this time, when he held out his hands, I quickly grabbed them and felt his warm embrace alongside the presence of Jesus. He spoke so much truth over me that day. Words of life, forgiveness, truth, and belief that God was going to give us a baby at the perfect time. He reminded me that because of *God's goodness,* nothing we've done can outrun His grace.

Brennan Manning shares with us the freedom of living out of a place of wholeness despite our wounds. He writes, "Without your wound where would your power be? It is your melancholy that makes your low voice tremble into the hearts of men and women. The very angels themselves cannot persuade the wretched and blundering children on earth as can one human being broken on the wheels of living. In Love's service, only wounded soldiers can serve. Physician, draw back."[3]

Every area means every area.

Through Jesus, God has made a way for us to be a recipient of wholehearted love.

What a kind, loving Father we have.

I woke up the next morning feeling so free, whole, and filled with the Spirit. It was a Sunday, and I couldn't wait to get to church to worship the Jesus who just continues to do such deep work of redemption in my life.

After leaving church, I had a random craving for Pringles. (I never eat Pringles.) So I pulled into the Walmart conveniently located right next to the church. I grabbed a sleeve of the sour cream and onion flavor (if you know you know) and, as I was leaving, I walked past the pregnancy tests and thought, *Should I take one?*

I was meeting Ryan and some friends for lunch, so I ran home, Pringles in hand (and mouth), and took the test as quickly as I could. If you have taken pregnancy tests before, you know that they can be a painful experience if you are trying to get pregnant. Negative test after negative test, waiting past the ten minutes "just in case," a positive sign shows up at the last second. But this time, God didn't even make me wait more than ten seconds before two clear blue lines showed up while my hand trembled.

I hit the ground and worshiped the God who is so big yet is in the business of redeeming our lives down to the very detail. Even with that pregnancy test that day, I see that He redeemed the dozens of negative tests in just one moment.

Friend, the timing of my confessing my past and finding out I was pregnant is no coincidence. God loves us *so* much that He allowed me to enter into my pregnancy season with no doubt of His love and forgiveness for me. In that moment, the day before, I was freed from the years of shame that I had carried over my sin. In an instant, I was healed. Not because I conceived a child, but because God showed up in the middle of my broken circumstances, and wrote a new story that traded death for life.

Friend, I want to acknowledge again that no two stories are the same. The painful reality is that some of you are still waiting and hoping for the miracle of a child or another unanswered prayer. If that's you, I want to encourage you that God is still writing a story. His story might not be the one you would write, but it is His version of good. A version that involves redemption, freedom, and life. A version where He shows up in the middle of your broken circumstances, reveals His tender heart for you, and writes a new story that gives Him all the honor and glory in the midst of our mess.

If you want this today, or if you want to go deeper into a life of wholeheartedness, I would encourage you to repent, which means to "turn away" from the things leaving you less than whole. Confess as I did, and receive as I did. The good news is that it's the Father's kindness that leads us to repentance, not His condemnation (Rom. 2:4).

It's His kindness and it's His *love* that give us a whole heart. What a whole hope we have today through the loving Father and the perfect Son.

radiant and redeemed

H ave you ever noticed an object that shines? I mean, *really* shines? I'm not talking about your friend who got a really solid spray tan in the winter from a Groupon she stumbled upon. I'm talking about a *radiance that cannot be hidden or mistaken for anything but God's goodness* kind of shine.

When Ryan asked me to marry him, saying yes was the easiest choice I ever made. As you know, we had been through so much and seen such abundant redemption together, and I knew this was who God had for me. I remember the moment he slipped the ring on my finger. It was the most beautiful symbol of love I had ever seen. That ring represented and still does today a commitment to sacrificially serve, seek to understand, and believe the best in each other as long as we both shall live.

It was a rainy New Year's Eve in Texas when I first slipped it on, but my ring didn't fail to bring an unexplained brightness to our night as we celebrated our future together with our families. We welcomed all that the New Year and our new life together had in store for us.

As adulting would have it, the memorable weekend ended, and Monday was calling my name. I returned to my office job, took a seat at my desk, and attempted to wrap my head around all that had happened and the changes that were coming for me that year. I was filled with gratitude to think of all that God had done to get us to that point. Even with my past, God was showing me that we can't outrun His love and that we are never too far gone to step back into the life He has prepared for us. That morning, I decided to take a quick walk before the demands of the day crowded my mind.

It was still early in the morning, but as the sun was rising, I knew it was going to be a beautiful day. I was soaking in this quiet moment when something amazing happened. I looked down at my ring, and it almost took my breath away. The light from the sun was hitting the diamond, and the brilliant shine that appeared was one I hadn't seen over the weekend. Not only did it have a new glow, the reflection of the ring shone in what seemed like endless directions. The morning sky seemed to reveal a deeper dimension. One that was there all along, but I hadn't seen it until that moment.

THE RECIPE FOR SHINE

I later discovered three factors work in unison to give diamonds their trademark shine: *reflection*, *refraction*, and *dispersion*.

Reflection is the process of light hitting the diamond surface and immediately bouncing back. Then the light goes deeper into the diamond, reaching into the ridges and filling those spaces with illumination. This is the *refraction* phase. Once refraction is completed, the light reaches beyond the diamond's interior and meets our eyes with a shine, and that is called *dispersion*. The shine created is radiant and multidimensional to the human eye and causes an internal awe that captivates the human heart.[1]

Friends, let us look at this process and consider what it means for us in light of the gospel as we prepare to move forward as redeemed and free daughters of the King.

1. The Light of Christ Will Have an Impact on Us

In John 8:12, Jesus says, "I am the light of the world. Whoever follows me will never walk in darkness, but will have the light of life" (NIV). This is a promise from Jesus that says whoever will let His light in them will not be the same. Just like the reflection in a diamond, the light that He offers doesn't have to be earned and isn't dependent on our performance, but will be freely and immediately given to whoever is willing to walk into His presence.

> Want to reflect His image? **Step into His presence and** let His life be your justification.

Another word for this is *justification*. Just like in a diamond, justification is an outside-in process. It can't be earned or strived for internally, but it can only come from the One who defeated death for us when we could do nothing for ourselves.

A lack of understanding of this reality was what had me caught up in my sin for years. I always thought I had to achieve to get to God, but that's not the gospel. The gospel tells us that it's just the opposite. We don't (and can't if we tried) have to get to God. God came to us through Jesus. He knew we couldn't reach Him, even with our best efforts. He descended to us, took on flesh, and lived the perfect life so that we could step into His accomplished work and reflect His image. And what is it that He asks us to do? Let *His life* be our boasting, knowing that our best efforts pale in comparison to the finished work of Christ.

A. W. Tozer says it better than I ever could: "Let the seeking man reach a place where life and lips join to say continually 'Be thou exalted,' and a thousand minor problems will be solved at once."[2]

Want to reflect His image? Step into His presence and let His life be your justification.

2. The Light of Christ Goes Deeper

The complete understanding and depth of who Jesus is will be a lifelong journey for me, but one thing I can tell you is Jesus is not interested in a one-time interaction. You are far more precious to Him than a quick, "Hello, nice to meet ya." No, He is interested in you. You on your good days, your bad days, with your past hurts, your habits, your quirks, and your fears. Jesus, by essence, is the Great Pursuer, and He will never stop being just that toward you. God called Jesus to go after the one, and as hard as it is to believe this, *you, my friend, are the one.*

As Jesus' light hits us, it will go into the cracks, corners, and hidden places of our life. Another word for this is *sanctification*. While justification is an outside-in, one-time accomplishment, sanctification is an inside-out invitation to let the light of Jesus in and change you.

Just as refraction in a diamond causes light to not discriminate against the dark places, Jesus will not discriminate against the dark places either. He doesn't have a threshold of how dark is too dark. In fact, He welcomes those places all the more. He is eagerly waiting for the opportunity to debunk this very lie in your heart. That lie that says because of what you've done in the dark, He will withhold His love and be unwilling to qualify you by His light. He will reach deeper until His light reaches every dark place inside of you.

One of my favorite people in the Bible is the apostle Peter. Peter represents all of us in some way. He was impulsive, quick to speak, sometimes seeing himself as better than he actually was. Peter wrestled with the temptation to give in to his natural sinful desires, and sometimes it got the very best of him. Sound familiar? Above all, I love Peter because, through his relationship with Jesus, we learn so much about how Jesus views us, even on our worst days.

Right before Jesus went to the cross, He let His disciples know during supper together that one of them was going to betray Him. Peter confidently declares that it definitely won't be him and that he would never do such a thing. Jesus quickly humbles His good friend by telling him that by the time the sun comes up, Peter will deny Jesus three times.

As the story goes, Peter follows Jesus and is brought into the high priest's courtyard. When faced with questioning about his affiliation with Jesus, all starts to go downhill.

"The servant girl at the door said to Peter, 'You also are not one of this man's disciples, are you?' He said, 'I am not.' Now the servants and officers had made a charcoal fire, because it was cold, and they were standing and warming themselves. Peter also was with them, standing and warming himself" (John 18:17–18).

Surrounded by the warmth of the fire, Peter's fear was also heating up that night. He goes on to deny Jesus two more times. Just as Jesus had said, the denials were followed by the rooster's crow and, as recorded, Peter "went out and wept bitterly" (Luke 22:62).

I think we've all been there when the reality of the ways we've turned away have hit us like a ton of bricks. Where the past feels so daunting and heavy that all we can do is run, hide, and feel the weight of our mistakes. But Jesus doesn't leave us there. It's there that His redemption actually starts.

Peter didn't get the opportunity to go to Jesus, apologize, and own what he had done before Jesus' death. I'm sure feeling like all was lost after his Savior, whom he had denied, was crucified, Peter must have had such a wide range of emotions. I can imagine that he thought it was all over and that perhaps he would never get the redemption his soul longed for.

So what did Peter do? He went fishing. While he was out on his boat looking for fish, he realized someone was simultaneously looking for him.

Just as day was breaking, Jesus stood on the shore; yet the disciples did not know that it was Jesus. Jesus said to them, "Children, do you have any fish?" They answered him, "No." He said to them, "Cast the net on the right side of the boat, and you will find some." So they cast it, and now they were not able to haul it in, because of the quantity of fish. That disciple whom Jesus loved therefore said to Peter, "It is the Lord!" When Simon Peter heard that it was the Lord, he put on his outer garment, for he was stripped for work, and threw himself into the sea. The other disciples came in the boat, dragging the net full of fish, for they were not far from the land, but about a hundred yards off.

When they got out on land, they saw a charcoal fire in place, with fish laid out on it, and bread. (John 21:4–9, emphasis added)

Did you catch that? The same place that Peter denied Jesus, a charcoal fire, was the exact place where Jesus wanted to have a specific chat with Peter. Was this the cruelty of Jesus to make Peter relive the events from the past that haunted him? No, it was a lifeline to show Peter that Jesus would do what we've been talking about this entire book: *redeem.*

It's the kindness of Jesus to recreate that scene for His friend. Otherwise, I believe that Peter would never see a charcoal fire the same after he denied Jesus. Before that day, whenever he saw one, he would replay the events that went down that cold night. The night he denied knowing his best friend, his teacher, his Savior. Peter would have been haunted by the imagery, and Jesus wasn't going to make His friend live a life subjected to shame and regret.

Not only did Jesus redeem the fire, but He redeemed each and every time Peter chose denial, offering him an opportunity for a new response.

When they had finished breakfast, Jesus said to Simon Peter, "Simon, son of John, do you love me more than these?" He said to him, "Yes,

Lord; you know that I love you." He said to him, "Feed my lambs." He said to him a second time, "Simon, son of John, do you love me?" He said to him, "Yes, Lord; you know that I love you." He said to him, "Tend my sheep." He said to him the third time, "Simon, son of John, do you love me?" Peter was grieved because he said to him the third time, "Do you love me?" and he said to him, "Lord, you know everything; you know that I love you." Jesus said to him, "Feed my sheep." (John 21:15–17)

Three denials. Three opportunities to claim the love of Jesus.

Jesus is not afraid of the dark parts. Just as light penetrates the dark corners of a diamond, Jesus penetrates the dark parts of our lives to create something beautiful and redeemed. Every area means every area, friend. Whatever your charcoal fire is, turn to Him and watch how He'll redeem it.

3. The Light of Christ Will Always Create a Shine in You

As you can see, there is a process to achieving a great shine. Psalm 34:5 reveals, "Those who look to him are radiant; their faces are never covered with shame" (NIV). Jesus bids our hearts to come and look. Taste and see. Step out and experience. This daily relationship based on love and trust is what produces in and through us a shine that disperses His light from the inside out, just like in the last phase of a diamond. This acts as a declaration to the world that we have been given a newness of purpose and identity in Christ.

> A life positioned in **the light of Christ** will be illuminated and bring to the surface who you've been all along.

A life positioned in the light of Christ will be illuminated and bring to the surface who you've been all along.

> The transformative work of Jesus is the recipe for a radiant shine.

You have always been seen.
You have always been loved.
You have always been lovely.
You have always been pursued.

Sometimes this is hard to believe because of things that have happened in our lives. Perhaps you've hidden sin and shame from God and others for a long time. You might think the decisions you've made have created a dull or damaged spirit, disqualifying you from this radiant life. If that's the case, God and diamonds have something to say about that.

Remember this about every shiny diamond you have ever "oohed" and "ahhed" over: even the shiniest diamonds are a collection of light and dark places. While this may seem like it would lessen the quality of the diamond's beauty, it is actually the thing that illuminates the shine.

If you think about it, a candle burns brightest not in a well-lit room, but in a poorly lit one. The same idea is true of diamonds. Diamonds aren't perfect, and those imperfections are what make them so breathtaking. The reason we are able to see the brightness of a diamond isn't from an absence of dark spaces, *but because of them.*

In one of his letters to the church in Corinth, Paul lets us in on a word that Jesus gave to Him on this matter: "But he said to me, 'My grace is sufficient for you, for my power is made perfect in weakness.' Therefore I will boast all the more gladly of my weaknesses, so that the power of Christ may rest upon me" (2 Cor. 12:9).

The transformative work of Jesus is the recipe for a radiant shine. No more, no less. He wants to redeem the darkest places in your life, and over time, those will be the areas that will give Him the most glory. God gave us the image of Himself through Christ that you and I might believe, be restored in relationship with Him, and be healed.

THE ULTIMATE INVITATION

The invitation God gave Adam and Eve in the garden after they sinned is the same invitation He extends to us today. When Adam and Eve tried to justify themselves with fig leaves, God offered a better covering. Years later, He would send His only Son to pay the penalty for our sin, giving us a better, eternal covering.

So many of us want to go back to the garden. While being naked and unashamed was once the norm for Adam and Eve, I'd like to argue we can have something even better. We can be fully who we are called to be under the covering and clothing of Christ. Full of freedom, redemption, and a representation of not going back, but looking to the future of His promised return. Until then, we are called to bring heaven down to earth by being willing to live as the redeemed.

John Mark Comer, in his book *Garden City*, explains our call as the redeemed children here on earth:

> We're called to a very specific kind of work. To make a Garden-like world where image bearers can flourish and thrive, where people can experience and enjoy God's generous love. A kingdom where God's will is done "on earth as it is in heaven," where the glass wall between earth and heaven is so thin and clear and translucent that you don't even remember it's there. *That's* the kind of world we're called to make.
>
> After all, we're just supposed to continue what God started in the beginning.[3]

What God started "in the beginning" was the greatest pursuit of love this world has ever seen, finally coming to fruition in Christ's life, death, and resurrection.

The blood of Jesus is our better covering.

Two thousand-plus years ago, Jesus saw you and me on the cross. He saw our sin, our past, our mistakes, our struggles, our shame, our regrets, our defeat, and our hopelessness. He looked upon our helpless state, and He had compassion on us. He was willing to take extreme measures to save us and restore us back to our original design: loved, freed, redeemed. This covering is available to us today. We don't have to take matters into our own hands. It is in great hands right where it is: *in His.* He is our hope for life change.

Manning's words speak to my heart when it comes to remembering Jesus is more than a good thought—He is our hope and our life. "The Christ within who is our hope of glory is not a matter of theological debate or philosophical speculation. He is not a hobby, a part-time project, a good theme for a book, or a last resort when all human effort fails. He is our life, the most real fact about us. He is the power and wisdom of God dwelling within us."[4]

Let's bring this full circle. The irony of a diamond's shine is that, scientifically, it's classified as a reflection rather than that of a shine. What beautiful, freeing news this is! Our shine is actually a reflection of *His pursuit of us.*

Find peace and rest in this, friends. Behavior modification is not needed for life change.

And as we reflect His image through His pursuit of us, we confess our sins, we live in the light, and we await His promised and glorious return where all will be redeemed once and for all in a new garden:

> Then the angel showed me the river of the water of life, bright as crystal, flowing from the throne of God and of the Lamb through the middle of the street of the city; also, on either side of the river, the tree of life with its twelve kinds of fruit, yielding its fruit each month. The leaves of the tree were for the healing of the nations. No longer

will there be anything accursed, but the throne of God and of the Lamb will be in it, and his servants will worship him. They will see his face, and his name will be on their foreheads. And night will be no more. They will need no light of lamp or sun, for the Lord God will be their light, and they will reign forever and ever. (Rev. 22:1–5)

This is the promise of the gospel. He is making *all* things new, including you. This promise is so beautiful, so captivating, and all we have to do is step into it and look up.

A. W. Tozer said it best: "Faith is a redirecting of our sight, a getting out of the focus of our own vision and getting God into focus."[5]

Reflect. Refract. Disperse. Repeat.

This is the hope we have—trading in fig leaves for Jesus.

acknowledgments

With this being my first book, I've learned many things along this journey. By far, one of the biggest lessons is just how much you need to have your people to write a book. And thank God, I did. To my tiny but mighty army of people who rallied around me to see this process through, thank you just doesn't cut it, but I will try.

First, thank You, Jesus. You carried me through this whole process as I wrote through pregnancy, pain, and deep dependence. You met me at the end of myself and showed me a path forward every time I was stuck. Thank You for calling me to write a book that also served as a tool for continued redemption in my own heart. Thank You for saving me and allowing me to share through these pages. I love You.

Ryan, what would I do without you? I could have never written this book if it wasn't for your wind in my sails on my hardest days. Thank you for actually reading my chapters after a long day of work and crying tears over these pages. I'm better in every way because of you. I believe women will find freedom because of your handprint on this book. I love you.

To my sons, Graham and Barrett, thank you for existing and allowing me the joy of being your mom. I've written parts of this book with both of you in my womb at this point, and each time I felt you kick, it was like you were cheering me on. I promise to do the same for you throughout your life as you live out all that God calls you to. I love you both so much.

To my family, thank you for believing in this message and celebrating with me throughout each milestone. Thank you for all the questions, check-ins, and genuine excitement over this book. You have shaped me more than you all know. Thank you for being my biggest cheerleaders. I'm so grateful to call each of you family.

To my friends, thank you for your unwavering support of this crazy dream. I have treasured every text, call, question, smile, moment of celebration, and pages read that made this book possible. If a person is a reflection of their people, you all make me look pretty good. I love each of you (you know who you are)!

To Crista, thank you for the countless hours of watching Graham so I could write this book. Your generous heart still amazes me, and I will never forget the way you have poured into this book by pouring into my son. I am forever grateful.

To Trillia, thank you for taking a chance on me. Some days I still wonder why (haha), but I couldn't have prayed for a better advocate for this message. Thank you for believing that these pages could bring people a little closer to Jesus.

To Ashleigh, your heart is all over this book. Thank you for every edit, every encouragement, every challenge, and every detail that you poured into making this book one hundred times better. Thank you for using your gift to be the biggest blessing to me and the reader. This book makes sense because of you, ha!

To my team at Faithfully Restored, thank you for actually living out freedom and redemption daily and offering it to others in the most tangible ways. I don't have the words to say how inspired I am by each of you, and I'm honored to be on your team.

To the team at Moody, thank you for letting me in to have a seat at this faith-filled table. Your pursuit of truth and the things of God is something I feel honored to be a tiny part of.

Lastly, to my dad. Thank you for modeling what a loving father was for me. Thank you for teaching me to open my Bible and to just take the next right step. I miss you every day, and I hope we can start a book club in heaven together one day. Thank you for letting me reflect your image. I love you forever.

notes

CHAPTER 1: AND IT WENT LIKE THIS . . .

1. J. M. Wheeler and G. W. Foote, *Voltaire: A Sketch of His Life and Works with Selections from His Writings* (London: Robert Forder, 1894), 88.
2. Brennan Manning, *Abba's Child: The Cry of the Heart for Intimate Belonging* (Colorado Springs: NavPress, 2015), 34.

CHAPTER 2: THE ORIGIN OF SHAME

1. David Guzik, "Genesis 3, Man's Temptation and Fall," *The Enduring Word Bible Commentary*, 2018, https://enduringword.com/bible-commentary/genesis-3/.
2. Ibid.
3. John Mark Comer, *Garden City: Work, Rest, and the Art of Being Human* (Grand Rapids, MI: Zondervan, 2017), 275–76.
4. James Finley, *Merton's Place of Nowhere: A Search for God Through Awareness of the True Self* (Notre Dame, IN: Ava Maria Press, 1978), 53.

CHAPTER 3: THE SECOND MOST POWERFUL FORCE ON EARTH

1. Jennie Allen, *Get Out of Your Head: Stopping the Spiral of Toxic Thoughts* (Colorado Springs: Waterbrook, 2020), 62.
2. Tchiki Davis, "Shame: Definition, Causes, and Tips," *Berkeley Well-Being Institute*, 2024, https://www.berkeleywellbeing.com/shame.html.
3. Brennan Manning, *Abba's Child: The Cry of the Heart for Intimate Belonging* (Colorado Springs: NavPress, 2015), 12.

CHAPTER 4: DEALING WITH FATHERHOOD WOUNDS

1. Jacqueline Tempera and Charlotte Walsh, "Meet Caitlin Clark's Family: What to Know About the Basketball Star's Parents and Two Brothers," *Women's Health*, April 15, 2024, https://www.womenshealthmag.com/life/a46696795/caitlin-clark-family/.
2. Steve Williams, *Crimson Ride* (Scotts Valley: Createspace Independent Pub, 2008), 208.
3. A. W. Tozer, *The Knowledge of the Holy* (San Francisco: HarperOne, 2009), 4.
4. Jen Wilkin, *In His Image: 10 Ways God Calls Us to Reflect His Character* (Wheaton, IL: Crossway, 2018), 148.
5. Ray Ortlund, "Don't Waste Your Fathering," The Gospel Coalition, January 5, 2016, https://www.thegospelcoalition.org/article/dont-waste-your-fathering/.
6. Trevin Wax, "Making Sense of Life After a Parent Leaves: A Conversation with Jonathan Edwards," The Gospel Coalition, September 16, 2014, https://www.thegospelcoalition.org/blogs/trevin-wax/making-sense-of-life-after-a-parent-leaves-a-conversation-with-jonathan-edwards/.

CHAPTER 5: DEALING WITH GOD WOUNDS

1. A. W. Tozer, *The Knowledge of the Holy* (San Francisco: HarperOne, 2009), 13.
2. Ibid., 98.
3. Ibid., 63.

CHAPTER 6: DEALING WITH DATING WOUNDS

1. *Mean Girls*, directed by Mark Waters, Paramount Pictures, 2004.
2. Matt Chandler, *The Mingling of Souls: God's Design for Love, Marriage, Sex, and Redemption* (Colorado Springs: David C Cook, 2015), 139.
3. Allie Beth Stuckey, *You're Not Enough (And That's Okay): Escaping the Toxic Culture of Self-Love* (New York: Sentinel, 2020), 9.
4. Ibid., 26.

CHAPTER 7: LETTING JESUS HEAL YOUR WOUNDS

1. Timothy Keller, *The Meaning of Marriage: Facing the Complexities of Commitment with the Wisdom of God* (London: Penguin Books, 2013), 62.
2. Alyssa Roat, "The Samaritans: Hope from the History of a Hated People." Bible Study Tools, updated May 17, 2024, https://www.biblestudytools.com/

bible-study/topical-studies/the-samaritans-hope-from-the-history-of-a-hated-people.html.

3. Alvin Lloyd Maragh, "The Healing Ministry of Jesus as Recorded in the Synoptic Gospels" (thesis, Loma Linda University, 2006), 457.

4. William Barclay, "Commentary on John 8," Study Light, https://www.study light.org/commentaries/eng/dsb/john-8.html.

5. A. W. Tozer, *The Pursuit of God* (Chicago: Moody Publishers, 2015), 61.

CHAPTER 8: WHY YOU NEED COMMUNITY

1. Dictionary.com, s.v. "harmony (*n.*)," https://www.dictionary.com/browse/harmony.

2. Brennan Manning, *Abba's Child: The Cry of the Heart for Intimate Belonging* (Colorado Springs: NavPress, 2015), 9.

3. *Oxford Advanced American Dictionary*, s.v. "empathy (*n.*)," https://www .oxfordlearnersdictionaries.com/us/definition/american_english/empathy.

4. Katie Stiles, "The Science of Tears," Psych Central, updated November 2, 2021, https://psychcentral.com/blog/the-science-of-tears.

5. Dane Ortlund, *Deeper: Real Change for Real Sinners* (Wheaton, IL: Crossway, 2021), 13.

6. Manning, *Abba's Child*, 12.

CHAPTER 9: HOW TO FINALLY FORGIVE YOURSELF

1. Charles Spurgeon, "The Perseverance of the Saints," The Spurgeon Center, May 23, 1869, https://www.spurgeon.org/resource-library/sermons/the-perseverance-of-the-saints/#flipbook/.

2. Dane Ortlund, *How Does God Change Us?* (Wheaton, IL: Crossway, 2021), 43.

CHAPTER 10: WHY WHOLENESS IS BETTER THAN PERFECTION

1. Robert Lowry, "I Need Thee Every Hour," 1872, https://hymnary.org/text/i_need_thee_every_hour_most_gracious_lor.

2. *Merriam-Webster*, s.v. "hope (*v.*)," https://www.merriam-webster.com/dictionary/hope.

3. Brennan Manning, *Abba's Child: The Cry of the Heart for Intimate Belonging* (Colorado Springs: NavPress, 2015), 12.

CHAPTER 11: RADIANT AND REDEEMED

1. Madhavi Deshpande, "Science Behind the Sparkling Brilliance of a Diamond," *Science ABC*, July, 8, 2022, https://www.scienceabc.com/pure-sciences/why-do-diamonds-sparkle.html.
2. A. W. Tozer, *The Pursuit of God* (Chicago: Moody Publishers, 2015), 69.
3. John Mark Comer, *Garden City: Work, Rest, and the Art of Being Human* (Grand Rapids, MI: Zondervan, 2017), 61–62.
4. Brennan Manning, *Abba's Child: The Cry of the Heart for Intimate Belonging* (Colorado Springs: NavPress, 2015), 130.
5. Tozer, *The Pursuit of God*, 60.

You finished reading!

Did this book help you in some way? If so, please consider writing an honest review wherever you purchase your books. Your review gets this book into the hands of more readers and helps us continue to create biblically faithful resources.

Moody Publishers books help fund the training of students for ministry around the world.

The **Moody Bible Institute** is one of the most well-known Christian institutions in the world, training thousands of young people to faithfully serve Christ wherever He calls them. And when you buy and read a book from Moody Publishers, you're helping make that vital ministry training possible.

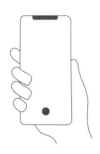

Continue to dive into the Word, *anytime, anywhere.*

Find what you need to take your next step in your walk with Christ: from uplifting music to sound preaching, our programs are designed to help you right when you need it.

Download the **Moody Radio App** and start listening today!